So a Child ?
Understands!

GARY R. MCCREE

WESTBOW
PRESS
A DIVISION OF THOMAS NELSON

WestBow Press books may be ordered through booksellers or by contacting:

WestBow Press
A Division of Thomas Nelson
1663 Liberty Drive
Bloomington, IN 47403
www.westbowpress.com
1-(866) 928-1240

Because of the dynamic nature of the Internet, any web addresses or links contained in this book may have changed since publication and may no longer be valid. The views expressed in this work are solely those of the author and do not necessarily reflect the views of the publisher, and the publisher hereby disclaims any responsibility for them.

Any people depicted in stock imagery provided by Thinkstock are models, and such images are being used for illustrative purposes only.

Certain stock imagery © Thinkstock.

ISBN: 978-1-4497-4309-3 (sc)
ISBN: 978-1-4497-4308-6 (hc)
ISBN: 978-1-4497-4310-9 (e)

Library of Congress Control Number: 2012904983

Printed in the United States of America

WestBow Press rev. date: 04/05/2012

So a Child ?
Understands!

GARY R. MCCREE

WESTBOW
PRESS
A DIVISION OF THOMAS NELSON

WestBow Press books may be ordered through booksellers or by contacting:

WestBow Press
A Division of Thomas Nelson
1663 Liberty Drive
Bloomington, IN 47403
www.westbowpress.com
1-(866) 928-1240

Because of the dynamic nature of the Internet, any web addresses or links contained in this book may have changed since publication and may no longer be valid. The views expressed in this work are solely those of the author and do not necessarily reflect the views of the publisher, and the publisher hereby disclaims any responsibility for them.

Any people depicted in stock imagery provided by Thinkstock are models, and such images are being used for illustrative purposes only.

Certain stock imagery © Thinkstock.

ISBN: 978-1-4497-4309-3 (sc)
ISBN: 978-1-4497-4308-6 (hc)
ISBN: 978-1-4497-4310-9 (e)

Library of Congress Control Number: 2012904983

Printed in the United States of America

WestBow Press rev. date: 04/05/2012

TABLE OF CONTENTS

Chapter 1.   Short Quotes.. 1
Chapter 2.   The Inspiration... 9
Chapter 3.   Poems.. 21
Chapter 4.   Short Quotes.. 39
Chapter 5.   My Proudest Moment 44
Chapter 6.   Poems.. 51
Chapter 7.   Short Quotes.. 60
Chapter 8.   The Little Man 66
Chapter 9.   Poems.. 74
Chapter 10.   The Atheist 81
Chapter 11.   Short Quotes.. 91
Chapter 12.   Poems.. 97
Chapter 13.   Short Quotes.. 110
Chapter 14.   Out of the Fire 118
Chapter 15.   Poems.. 127
Chapter 16.   Short Quotes.. 134
Chapter 17.   Poems.. 139
Chapter 18.   Short Quotes.. 150
Chapter 19.   Poems.. 154
Chapter 20.   Short Quotes.. 161
Chapter 21.   The Light Is Not Black or White 166

Introduction

This book is the end result of a year off to reflect on the thoughts and choices of one life. Prepare to search deeper than usual to find what is hidden under the surface. It's easy to see what stands before us. It is much more difficult to try to see the meaning of what stands before us and how it came to be. Only my wife of thirty years who stood by my side has witnessed the things I'm about to share. I have been blessed my whole life to a point where at times I feel guilty to be so blessed. I have often wondered why, especially when I see someone who, through no fault of their own, endured unbelievable hardships. Few people have spent so much time figuring out why things are so good as I have. Most I talk to are trying to figure out why things are so bad. The more I studied the farther back I had to dig. When I started understanding what led me here, I felt the need to share this with others. I turned to Him for advice and knew it needed to be in the simplest terms to reach the most hearts and minds. I struggled, as most do, to find big impressive words I decided just to put it in the simplest of forms. This is an attempt to introduce you to God as one man was introduced to Him: in a manner a child understands.

SHORT QUOTES

Here's a thought; seems like everyone wants you to pick their side and fight with them. Put an end to the fighting. To each his own! Next time pick both sides and walk away.

I think my favorite quote that has always stuck with me is "I have never met a man I didn't like but I've come to know a few" . . . . Will Rodgers.

I love people who love people!

Who could have known His words of tolerance would spark so much controversy. Ironic isn't it?

Just like a child who misbehaves His words only frighten those who choose to disobey Him.

Take some time for yourself, do for yourself, give too yourself and like yourself knowing He will. That's why He made you!

Judge another then you must judge yourself and you have already failed.

If you have to know someone before you can love them you want to judge them worthy of your love. Maybe you're not worthy of theirs.

Time is a one-way street!

I know I don't have the answers for another. Rarely do I have my own. Trying to live the things I write has worked well for me.

When your mind is confused just tell it to follow the heart and the heart will lead you to the answers the mind needs.

These thoughts come like a tornado passing through the mind spitting out bits and pieces as it passes.

I'd rather walk or stand with God than run like the Devil.

Have you noticed the weather is the news lately? He's talking to us!

I understand the feeling of revenge. I have found it to be better and sweeter to sit back and watch Him take care of it.

Where would you be without everyone before you and Him? Nowhere!

Acts of kindness in the future can make up for bad acts in the past. A lot to do; better get started!

You say you're not happy? Go put a smile on a child's face and I bet you won't be able to wipe the one off yours.

While you were sitting here complaining to me about it you could have done something about it.

If you have been trying your best to make someone happy and it becomes obvious they don't want to be. Leave them alone and they will come around.

If you were handed a hundred dollars for one meal would you dress up and treat yourself to a hundred dollar steak or take ninety nine friends out for dollar burgers?

How much love we receive from others is determined by how much love we give to others. How much do you want?

Unlike UFO's, Bigfoot and ghosts that people constantly try to prove exist and can't, God is something people constantly try to prove doesn't exist and can't.

I've seen several people who didn't believe change their mind. I've never seen people who truly believe change theirs.

If you wish to achieve new heights reach higher!

You can flap your jaws all day, it doesn't mean you are saying anything.

Watching and listening is learning. Speaking puts an end to that.

Do you do things to be appreciated or because you appreciate?

I wonder how many men have been imprisoned for breaking a questionable law of man but broke no law of God? I'm glad I wasn't the one who took their freedom. I have a feeling there is a big price to pay for that.

I thought I could; now I know I can.

You're His son or daughter! Don't you think it's time you act like it and help your brothers and sisters?

I've been told this could bring attacks from the Devil. We've gone a few rounds in the past and I'm still standing!

If you choose to disagree that is your right. If you choose to fight about it I won't. I win!

Don't give in, give out or give up! Just give!

I learned to crawl and only wanted to walk. I learned to walk and only wanted to run. Now I've stopped running, started walking with Him and go back to my knee's to give Him praise.

You will find your heart is where it belongs when you give it to others.

I've tried stopping but my mind won't.

I thought I was smart until I realized it was my stupid mistakes and others wisdom that led me to the answers.

The right one will see you as perfect just the way you are and encourage you to do the same.

Everyone is a diamond in the rough. Even you! Good luck finding a polished one just waiting to be found.

Force your kids to be who you want them to be and it will keep you from knowing the beauty of whom and what they really are.

When we realize we are not perfect we get a lot closer to perfection.

What comes around goes around. What were you expecting?

Happiness is a choice! Stop whining and chose it!

What makes it so difficult is the fact we don't realize we are blind until we see.

100% guarantee; the best choices are made with His advice.

Striving to be a better person and helping others has become the most addictive thing I do.

If I had the time I would list all the things that made me believe in fifty years of living. Trust me neither one of us have the time.

Life! Can't control it! Stop trying! What happened to worry? It left with control!

Trying to make a monkey out of him will make a monkey out of you.

These thoughts are shallow for a reason. Everyone can wade but some can't swim.

If nothing in here makes you smile pull my finger.

I've been listening for years. Your turn!

If you think I take myself too seriously then you are missing who these words take seriously.

It's easy to keep from being disappointed in others. Don't expect anything!

I've found some of the brightest lights in the darkest places.

A lie might get you through today, but it will take you down tomorrow.

If you spend all your time talking about yourself, thinking about yourself, worrying about yourself and doing for yourself, odds are you will end up by yourself.

If you haven't found the joy in helping others then I bet you haven't found much joy period have you?

Everyone matters when they choose to!

Stop acting like you didn't know better!

You can make a change today that will change the lives of great, great, great, great grandchildren a hundred years from now. If that doesn't make you want to do better then nothing will.

It takes less than one minute to touch a heart and make a smile.

How do you know if you truly are a good person, parent, friend, spouse, lover, giver or anything else? Listen! It's most true when spoken of you not by you!

People ask me why I think kids love me. I think it's because I love them.

Are you a kid for your kids as often as you ask them to be an adult for you?

Taking time for your kids will do as much for you as it will for them.

Why do we demand our kids to act like adults while as adults we constantly look for ways to feel like a kid again?

Would your child go into shock if you told them thank you?

You tell me you won't apologize first for the disagreement you have with someone. I ask you: when did you stop wanting to be the (a) better person?

Have you ever noticed the harder you work to keep your cool the harder some work to get you to loose it?

It's your choice sit and wait for Him to come to you or get up and go to Him. Time is wasting!

The best things in life are free and they all came through Him.

We are all born innocent, giving and loving. It's the so-called adults that start screwing it all up.

If you don't love life then I bet you're not living it.

What's the difference between a humanitarian and a terrorist? God!

You don't find love looking. It finds you living!

How hard is it to find love? Smile!

It's better to think and do than do and think!

I thought I had all the answers. I was wrong. I thought I found them in someone else. Once again, I was wrong. When I found His words and put them to work in my life I finally started to get it right.

The only thing to fear is a life without knowing Him!

THE INSPIRATION

I have stopped to study the things that I've written and how they came to be several times while writing this book. Sometimes I stopped to wonder why I was writing it at all. I've always believed in God. I never felt the need to sit down and do what I'm doing now. I have always felt that I have been led to and guided through this project by Him. Even that feeling didn't satisfy my constant need to understand, though. The more I worked on this project and the more time I took to think about it, the more I understood about how I came to feel this way. The more I talked to people about what I was doing, the more I realized how important it was and to how many. The more I wrote, the more I understood, so the more I wrote, and so on and so on. The more of it I shared, the more I was encouraged to keep going. It became some kind of snowball rolling down a mountain faster and faster.

The year 2010 will always be referred to as the year of the women in my life. I have always loved and respected women. Never before did they consume so much of my time. Four of the most important women in my life all came to need me at the same time. My wife, my mother-in-law, my daughter, and my new grandbaby all needed my best at the same time. This was one time I couldn't fail. They had all been there for me throughout the years. I had been there for them over the years, but mostly in little ways. The problems they all faced now were big, and everything mattered.

The year began with our young daughter, four months pregnant with her first child—a very scary time for anyone in that position. My wife and I were committed to helping her in every way possible. She needed our support more than ever. When I think of all the young girls who didn't get the support they needed, it makes me very grateful for our decision to help. When your baby is having a baby, life becomes even more intense than when you yourself are having one. Every doctor's appointment, cold, sniffle, heartbeat, and moment seem magnified. Every parent knows all the preparations that go into bringing home a new life. It seemed every day that went by that my daughter grew more apprehensive, as well as my wife.

It would be wrong not to include myself as growing more apprehensive every day too.

On May 31—Memorial Day, 2010—our daughter went into labor one month early. Talk about adding to the stress! Everything became tenser very quickly. Not just for us, but for the doctors and nurses also. Our daughter did remarkably well. On the day people stopped to remember lost loved ones our beautiful granddaughter was born. A special baby was born on a special day.

There was very little time to celebrate. All vital signs were very good, but she only weighed five pounds. She was so small, yet so beautiful. Special attention was given to her because of her size. It was scary at the time, but all the while, with God watching over her. She did fine. They put her in the pre-natal care unit for a few days. We could only go in two at a time to be with her. Those five or six days, she had a constant line of visitors. We had to scrub for three minutes but no one minded. Our daughter was a very protective mother, and her instincts took over. Just as in labor, she began her mothering skills like a seasoned veteran. Most of the credit for that go to her mother and grandmother.

Every day we left the hospital feeling love and inspiration. We were very blessed and happy. Unfortunately my mother-in-law was slipping away at the same time. The mood would quickly change when we got home. My wife would check in on her mom, and good feelings where replaced with feelings of sorrow and pain. It was a very emotional time in our life, to say the least. About the same day my beautiful grandbaby was being brought home, my beautiful mother-in-law was being prepared for a nursing home. Every day it seemed that while things were going well for one, the other would be going through some kind of difficulty. This was very stressful for my wife. It also became very stressful on our relationship. There was a point when it seemed we were meeting ourselves coming and going. Never before had our life together been so little about us and so much about others. It's funny how the business is what got us through that rough time. There was no time to stop and think about anything. There was always something else that needed done.

The better the situation got with our two babies, the worse things got for my wife and her mom. We rode the emotional rollercoaster and took every minute as it came. Before we realized it, the year was half over, and it was hard to make sense of everything that was happening. With my busy time being in the winter, I was very fortunate to have plenty of time to be there for my family. I spent most of my time visiting with our daughter and helping her by babysitting. We went to several doctor appointments together, and it was a real bonding experience for both of us. The time I got to spend with our new granddaughter was priceless.

The best part for me was being able to be home when my wife was home and let her know I would be there. We all know there is nothing we can do or say when these situations arise. The only thing one can do is be there, which is not always easy. When you are the one who truly is there, you will usually be the person feelings and emotions are taken out on. Our worthiness as a true friend is in our ability to take these emotions head on without lashing back. *It's not easy sometimes* would be an understatement.

My wife also had the added stress of having just started a new job. She worked for this company and had known these were good people for some time. Anyone who knows my wife will tell you she will not settle for less than her best, but it's hard to give your best with so many distractions. So it no longer mattered how good the people or her new job was, it became another monumental stress for her to deal with daily. For me, the hardest part of the whole deal was watching how much pressure was placed on her at once. Such a wonderful person should not be beaten on constantly, which is what I was watching take place. Her pain became my pain. We have always been funny that way. When one of us gets a toothache, the other one gets a toothache. Watching her endure pain that was almost too much for her to bear was too much for me to bear. She talked to her mom every night, and I knew when she hung up that it was coming. I never knew which emotion it would be, but I knew it was coming.

In late August, we were told her mom had one to three months to live. Even though we knew her time was limited, it was hard to hear such news.

Fall was fast approaching, and my busy season was on the way. I had been there every minute up to that point for all four of them. Every time one of them called not only did I answer, but I showed up. I quickly learned that was a luxury few get to experience. Other than the normal problems that arise trying to raise a child, things with our two babies was going pretty smoothly. Our new granddaughter was bringing such unbelievable joy into our home. We spent time talking to friends, and even managed to share laughs with one another, but, the only real joy came through our daughter and granddaughter. It seemed the rollercoaster was getting faster with higher peaks and steeper drops. We wanted to get off, but there was no sign of it stopping anytime soon.

I made the decision to cut back on my responsibilities at the club, which isn't easy when you own and operate it. I decided I would book no weekends and only work through the week while my wife was working. I also decided anyone who wanted to come would have to be willing to leave early so I could be home when she got there. Weekends were a busy time, and we both knew this would have a major effect on our income. For me, it wasn't about money. I don't know if I would have done it any differently even if she had wished me to. I'd made a commitment to myself as much as to her to be there, and that was what I intended to do. It was still three months to the actual start of season, and as bad as her mom's condition was I didn't think she would still be with us when hunting season came. I put off all preparations so I could be there for all of them. Sometimes being there for our daughter was the best way to take some of the stress off my wife. To me it didn't matter what they wanted or needed me to do, it was just a matter of being there to do it. Never in my life have I witnessed so many extreme mood changes in such little time. I often wonder today how we ever made it through all that and still came out of it in love. I think that season of life is a testament to just how strong our love has grown in the thirty-three years since we met.

Sometimes it feels like our best efforts to help the ones we love are done in vain. These are the times people most often turn to God seeking his wisdom and help. I found myself turning to him more than ever do to what was happening. Watching them get progressively worse is probably the most difficult thing we do during our life. Everyone handles these situations differently. I witnessed that no matter how we handle it, we all need every moment of support we can get. I found myself praying for all four of these beautiful women on a daily basis. You should know I do not attend regularly at any specific church. I don't walk around with a bible preaching the word. I have participated in very few forms of organized religion. At the same time I would put my faith up against anyone's. I have always felt His Word is something you do twenty-four/seven. I'm in His church when I'm outdoors, at home or with family and friends. It's something you live. It's not something you practice or need reminded of; it's just what you do. Time spent studying The Word and time spent with others who believe it have worked best for me.

We didn't expect to spend Thanksgiving with Ma. We did and were grateful to be able to, but it was bitter sweet. When a body shuts down while the mind and heart are still strong, it can be a long journey. As Ma's condition worsened so did my wife's. Their bond as mother and daughter was as strong as any I have ever witnessed. Throughout this process I learned the deeper love runs the deeper the pain that comes with their passing. This pain was big and seemed to get worse everyday. People who know will tell you I have a pretty high tolerance for pain. I've found my biggest weakness to be watching the ones I care about the most going through pain. For the first time I was feeling a pain deeper than any ever before. What was strange was how it was coming to me through sympathy for others. I've never in thirty-two years together watched my wife hurt so deeply for so long. That was the hardest part for me.

By this time health was no longer an issue for our daughter or granddaughter. At least, no more than the normal worries that all parents face. Something amazing was taking place with our two babies. They were bonding and falling in love with each other. We were all amazed at the effort or daughter was making at being a good mom. I have to admit, I had my doubts. I remember telling my wife we would have to raise this baby, because our daughter wasn't ready to be a mom. She was just getting into her own life. Not necessarily the right life either. She could be, well, I'll just say a little selfish and spoiled. One of my prouder moments as a father was when she asked me if I ever thought she would turn out to be a good mom. I told her I had my doubts, but I was very proud of the way she had changed her life to revolve around her baby. I had to smile when she said that to me. It was a great feeling to see her as proud of herself as I was of her.

It seemed no matter how hard we tried to keep things on the lighter side the more that would come upon us. This was going to prove to be one of our biggest tests. Smiles could be wiped away with a phone call. The strange part was the greater the blessing that made us smile, the worse the phone call would be that followed.

In the middle of all this hunting season had started, but I felt I couldn't leave the house. It seemed every time I would have people come in and head to the farm, I would get a phone call insinuating I should be home. I've done a lot of traveling and had to spend several days away from home. Never before was I so torn to walk out the door. Somewhere between Thanksgiving and Christmas we decided to shut down the guide service all together. It was a decision that was difficult to make. When you have a little over four months to do most of your business for the year, you know everyday counts. Shutting down the whole season is giving up a year's salary. It was something we struggled with the whole season. I've never regretted the decision but I knew it was going to add to the stress. I found it to be a point in my life where it didn't matter what you did; it wasn't going to fix anything. The most difficult part of dealing with the club was explaining our situation to everyone as the calls came in.

When the New Year began Ma was still hanging on and everything seemed to be in a holding pattern. We were commuting the two-hour drive back and forth. Trying to give my wife as much time as possible with her mom was the objective. For our daughter it was more about daily survival. We helped as much as possible with rent, utilities, vehicle costs and baby supplies. Most of the time, this wouldn't have been difficult, but with the club shut down, it was a strain on our finances to say the least. Gas money alone back and forth was adding up quick. It seemed there were no good answers to any of the situations we were facing. At the same time I noticed the work load inside and outside the house was becoming all mine. Everyday that went by we basically were just waiting for and expecting a phone call. At one point my wife likened it to going to a funeral for six months. That probably described our emotional situation better than anything.

All the while, we are trying to enjoy our new grandbaby and go on about our business. We didn't know what we would be facing from one minute to the next. In thirty years of marriage we have never faced so much at once. I was so proud of my wife. She never let on. For the most part she went about her business as she always does. Few people saw her break down even though she had reason to almost every single minute of every single day. I was starting to see through all of this just how blessed I was. My wife, my daughter and my grandbaby were all showing great courage, strength and ability: everything anyone could ever dare ask for from his family. In our darkest hours I was proud to be a husband, a father and a grandpa. It's strange how tragedy will often bring out our best and bring things to light that have been standing right before you the whole time without being seen.

Sometime in January the mood started changing about Ma. She had reached a point of such great pain and inability that we knew it wasn't going to get better. Conditions now made it way too obvious. My wife referred to her mom's condition as existing, not living. I think existing might even have been stretching it a little. It's hard to believe that you can love someone so much, and still, in a strange way, be looking forward to his or her passing. We are not the first to be in such a dire situation and I know some of you can understand what I am trying to say. None of us wanted to see her go but at the same time none of us could bare to see her in such a horrible state any longer. You know when it gets to that point it is getting bad. I can only speak for myself, but as for me, I had as much difficulty watching my wife and her siblings suffer as I did Ma. It's just one of those times in life when we do what we got to do even though we know the end results won't change.

Ma held on for six months after the doctors told us one to three. The last three months my wife lay by her side and stroked her hair. I would sit at the foot of the bed and rub her feet and calves. In the middle of all this I was noticing a change taking place in us that I still have a hard time explaining to this day. It seemed the situations in our life had started to change all of us. I was reprioritizing my life to the point nothing else mattered. My wife was showing amazing strength and courage. My daughter had grown into a beautiful adult and mother. My mother-in-law, a true angel on Earth, was being called home to all the angels called before her.

You may be starting to notice this story bounces back and forth between happy and sad. That time in my life brought life and death, joy and sorrow, light and dark in magnified quantities. This story bounces back and forth just like the emotions we were experiencing in our lives. Our grandbaby has been the only thing to hold us all together. She brings smiles to us with her presence and we use that to our advantage as much as possible. When she came home from the hospital and we all knew she was doing fine, I don't remember one second that we have not been in joy in her presence. She truly is a gift to us from God. That little baby has accomplished so much without even knowing. She has been the only thing to keep Grandma smiling and I have to say Grandpa can't give enough thanks for that. Not even a year old, and she has brought more joy and happiness into the world then some of us will in a lifetime. I look forward to the day when I can tell her how much she has done for all of us.

Sometime during the last month Ma was still with us she went through a time of great fear. She sobbed like a little child and clung to her baby. Her sobbing and shaking were so real that she struggled for her breath. I was never more proud of my wife than I was that day. She stayed so strong for her mom. They talked of God and Pop, who had passed a few years before. My wife found words to comfort her mother when there really were no words. The whole thing was too much for both of us. I rarely ask for anything from God. My life has been so blessed I have very little reason to ask or even expect more in my life. Usually, when I do ask a favor, it is for someone else I care about. For some reason on this day I felt the need to go to the cemetery where Pop was and Ma soon would be. I stood there and, for the first time in my life, spoke out loud in front of a headstone hoping to reach the other side with my words.

I stated that I knew Pop could see how much pain Ma was in. I knew he could see she was scared and having doubts about death. I asked God if he could send his angels to comfort her, and maybe He could allow Pop to get a message to her so she would feel more at ease. I told Pop he had not and would not be forgotten. I then thanked him for all he had taught me during his time here. I promised to love and take care of his babies to the best of my abilities. I thanked God for all he had given me and promised to do my best. As I headed back to the truck I felt a calm peaceful feeling inside that gives me chills right now just to think about it.

When I returned back to the nursing home I was relieved to find ma sleeping with my wife lying next to her. The mood in the room had changed, but not much was said at that time. I didn't tell my wife about going to the cemetery. The strange thing was, the next few times we saw Ma she didn't exhibit any fear at all. Now she was saying things trying to comfort all of us. It was a complete turn around from the week before. Late one night on the way home my wife commented on the fact that she thought the talk her and her mom had really eased her mind. She asked if I had noticed the change in her since that day. That's when I told her about the talk I had the same day at the cemetery. I mentioned some beautiful orange flowers that someone had taken out there and she said, "Oh my God you did go out there, didn't you?" It gave us both chills when we compared the things we had said and done. Maybe neither one of us had anything to do with Ma's peace but it sure was an amazing transformation. It sure got our attention.

As the year passed by, I was finding myself changing the things that mattered to me. Things that had meant something my whole life suddenly didn't mean anything. The only thing that mattered was family. The day came when we got that phone call we knew was coming. Ma had passed. Even though the call was expected, it wasn't any easier to take. I rushed to my wife and we returned home just to be together. Once again, many emotions ran through us as we reflected on everything that had taken place. We were both saddened by her passing but strangely relieved that she was no longer suffering. The bond between two people is never more evident than with the loss of one of the two. The other is left with a pain that runs every bit as deep and true as the love they shared. Ironically, I had sent a poem to my wife and her sisters two days before she passed. I had no idea what that poem was going to lead to.

Because of that poem, my wife's sister asked me if I would mind doing Ma's eulogy. I immediately said yes, but I remember having doubts as I did so. Ma was such a wonderful person who had touched many people in her life, and I didn't know if I could do her life justice, let alone the fact I didn't feel like the best person for the job. That night I sat down and began writing about another's life. I don't think anyone can foresee the responsibility that comes with such a task until you sit down and attempt to do it. You struggle to find words that describe someone in a way that everyone can relate. It's not just what you feel, but you have to try to understand how others feel as well. I spent two long nights sitting by myself writing. The whole time I was learning things about myself as well as Ma. The loss of a loved one is a spiritual experience in itself. Throw in a project like a eulogy and it becomes life changing.

On the day we carried Ma to her final resting place, I stood before her family and friends to speak of the great life she had lived. I had written three different versions but decided not to use any written words and just speak from the heart. I know it must be hard to understand how the whole experience changed me forever, but it did. As I stood facing all those people who were all looking at me, it was like I could feel the pain and the love felt by everyone in that room. For a moment, all that emotion was directed to me. I could feel it deep inside my soul. All the experiences in my life had never touched or moved me in such a way. The words I spoke came from the heart, and, at times, I felt they were being sent to me from above. I will be the first to admit that sounds strange, but it is as true as me sitting here writing this book. When it was over I felt a sense of satisfaction. Before anyone had a chance to say anything I felt confident that Ma would have been pleased. As people came up and complimented me on the words I had spoken, I had an overwhelming feeling of comfort.

What happened next was this book. From the day Ma passed all I had thought about was love and where it originates. The same connection I felt writing Ma's eulogy was still stirring me up inside. I was hungry for answers, and I felt the need to keep writing. I wrote for six weeks. Day and night I wrote about Ma, family, love, friends, death, life and anything else that seemed to be connected to all the emotions everyone was feeling. I couldn't stop writing. At times I felt like I was being encouraged from somewhere else. As I wrote I felt like it was helping me put things into perspective. I started thinking about how we all struggle with these situations and wanted to explain how I came to believe so strongly. I started hoping that I could maybe help someone else get through tough times and find his or her own piece of mind. Every thought in this book came to me in a six-week period. My wife watched in amazement; I couldn't write the thoughts down fast enough. Unable to type fast enough I had to write it all down with pen and paper. It took two weeks of nonstop typing to load it all in the computer.

I'm not sure what has taken place to change me in such a way. All I know for sure is I don't feel like the same person. I have always believed, but never in such a way as I do now. I tell people I used to believe, but now I know. I know I would have never sit down to write these words without going through the whole experience. My wife and my friends will tell you they see a difference in me too. The changes have all been good. It seems to have magnified my beliefs as well as my love and appreciation for life. Even though the thoughts kind of jump around a bit, it is easy to see how things have come together for me. When I started adding it all up, I was left with a feeling of peace in my heart. Even though we had just gone through one of our toughest years, I felt a calming sensation that has stuck with me everyday since.

I wish to leave you with something to think about. This one fact alone amazed me when I sat down and took the time to study our lives together. Eighteen years ago my wife became pregnant with our daughter. We waited nine months for her birth. Nine months after our daughter was born we lost my wife's father. It was our shared love for our daughter that got us through that difficult time. Eighteen years later our daughter became pregnant. Once again we waited for nine months for the birth of our grandbaby. Nine months to the day after her birth we lost my wife's mother. It has been that beautiful grandbaby that has gotten us through these most difficult times. Now you can dismiss this fact anyway you choose. As for us, we know without a doubt that He knew we were going to need those two beautiful baby girls to get through. Eighteen months before the worst two loses of our life He sent us a blessing to get us through each one. I have no doubt that as close as my wife was to her parents, it would have destroyed us without those babies to hold us together. I have no doubt that He knew this as well. There is ten years between our two kids because of two miscarriages after our first child. We had pretty much given up hope of having another one all together. Not only was the timing of our daughter's arrival a blessing, but the very fact she arrived at all was more than just a blessing; it was a miracle.

When my wife and I talk about our life together now, we know we are not responsible for our success. We have been guided in a way that has always kept us together and in love with each other. No one will ever convince me that my life wasn't blessed before it even began. God's love was passed to us after being passed down through generations. We will gratefully spend the rest of our days trying to make sure it gets passed on to others.

I feel very blessed that I was in a position where I could drop everything to just be where I was needed. Not many have that opportunity. Not only was it meaningful time spent with family, but it gave me time to look back on my life. It takes a lot of time to really take a good look at the things you have done in your life. I have always been proud of the type of person I am and the real desire I have to help others. For some reason now I don't seem to feel like I can do enough. When you begin to realize how important every thought, action, word and especially time is, you don't want to waste one second. The weirdest thing of all is it has nothing to do with what I can do for myself or my so-called "bucket list". It has more to do with what I can do for others in however much time I have left here. The soul purpose for writing this book was the thought of being able to lay the groundwork for at least one more person to see as clearly as I now do.

The year of the women in my life will certainly not soon be forgotten. I sit here now amazed at the fact that the one year in my life most would think I would want to forget is the one year I wish to remember the most. They say, *what doesn't kill us only makes us stronger.* I would have to say this is very true in my case. I don't think I have ever grown so much in a year in my life. I know that even though I believed in His word my whole life, never before have things been so clear. I think when Ma left us she took some of the things I needed to lose with her. At the same time I think our new grandbaby brought the one thing we needed: love. The only thing I have ever felt in that little girl's presence is love. Although this one story alone could be looked at as a coincidence. I don't think you can put all these thoughts and stories together without at least stopping to think about it. I know some will refuse to believe no matter what, and to those I say you have your right. As for me I no longer believe, I know.

This Book

To sum this all up with a little word
Mostly God's love is what will be heard
Next most important to keep your mind open
That is for all to help with the copin'
Important things we all can learn
Short cuts to wisdom we don't have to earn
Try to find God that is the mission
His love received instead of just wishin'
Every last quote along with each story and poem
In hope at least one might get you to know him
Thoughts of one man and what he's been through
Written in words to present a new view
Purposely simple would be the intention
Getting difficult to understand this is the prevention
In some ways for children it's a simple read
Information for all to sow a good seed
I feel all these words to be heaven sent
I know that's why with them I'm so content
Read every line and look in-between
All the messages told so the thought could be seen

THIS HOUSE

This house was built with love
He passed it down from above
Gives us a new solid foundation
That's the backbone of creation
Four walls and a roof provide
Protection from the storms outside
Windows to let the light in
So to see we will begin
With rooms it becomes a home
In here comfort we can roam
The house that gives him praise
Good children it did raise
Where there should be no fright
For those that sleep at night
It helps keep the winters warm
Solid lives begin to form
For everyone it is the place
To come and share in his grace
Doors open wide for all
No need to ask, no need to call
As I sit here all alone
I know I'm thankful to the bone
Now it's quiet as a mouse
I'm so thankful for this house

NIGHTTIME LULLABY

Piercing the darkness and breaking the still
The lonesome song of the whippoorwill
A solitary hoot the wise old owl
The coyote looks up and begins to howl
Travel by the stars, birds in flight
Marking their passing songs in the night
The frogs keep time rhythm all around
Some in the trees others on the ground
A beaver slaps his tail like a big bass drum
Even the mosquito, you can hear him hum
The leader of the band the lonely cricket
This song is free, you don't need a ticket
So much to see but not with the eye
Filling your ears with what, where and why
Tiny little critters you can hear them chatter
Looking for a meal, nothing else will matter
The wind is the background, tempo and score
It may only whisper, sometimes it will roar
God is the composer, he wrote this nights song
To teach in the dark, we can still get along
Listen every night before you go to bed
Written for you, sweet sounds fill your head
Close your eyes and let out a peaceful sigh
Calm comes to all through his nighttime lullaby

A Poem to Heaven

The most meaningful words that I'll ever write
Are the ones I'll put on this paper tonight
Already knowing no man will ever be able
To put down in words what you brought to the table
The creator of earth and its atmosphere
Your love all I see, your voice all I hear
From the beginning to this very minute
Every act of kindness I see your heart in it
All carried out by those who honor your name
They refuse to let your work be done in vain
Through thousands of years and all generations
Your love for each life as well as all nations
I've spent time tracking love back to its start
Every single time I was led back to your heart
It didn't take me long now I can understand
All the love here today came from your hand
Handled with care passed down with belief
Providing comfort, care, hope and relief
I know my life has been blessed with your glory
Why I feel compelled to help spread your story
Rarely with words does my mind struggle
I try to place these to help complete the puzzle
I wish there was someway to write a book
Everyone could open it and take a good look
Listing every name that believed in you
Each name with a list how you got them through
Pages bound together stack up through the clouds
Nothing since Jesus would draw so many crowds
A thousand lifetimes to compile the information
A thousand lifetimes to read of true destination
It would take the strength of many to pick it up
Just stories of someone filling another's cup

Each story proudly stating how credit is yours
Living proof out of our heart your love pours
Sorrow for the lost who know not what they do
Kick you out of school, keep you far from view
They can't believe they say there's not enough proof
Bet I can find you under their very own roof
I'd ask them to imagine the book in my dreams
A book of love that is bursting at the seams
Imagine the lost who think they know better
Than millions before who believed to the last letter
I hope this poem helps at least one lost soul find
With your love in our heart troubles will unwind
It's never to late to start reflecting your light
The only guarantee we'll get back any delight
But if we are waiting for the love you are serving
First we must show you that we are deserving
That's when we'll see mountains start moving
Our life here with others becoming more soothing
We will find the knowledge to pass every test
We will no longer settle for less than our best
I could go on and on until my very last day
I can't believe you come to my house to play
I look straight in your eyes every single week
I couldn't believe it when you kissed me on the cheek
Every day you've been here our home filled with laughter
I saw you before now I'll see you until the ever after
Surprised I don't see you as much at the altar
I see you grin in the smile of my granddaughter

YOUR BOOK OF LIFE

If you wrote a book describing your life
Would it make you proud or add to the strife?
Would it be filled with wisdom and love?
A life smiled upon when examined from above
Filled with stories of the times you cared
Shouting out with honor, all the gifts you shared
The book you are writing, how bright is your star
Are all the minds pages true of who you are?
Do the words on those pages take others far?
Every book would be different in so many ways
The things we all chose to fill all our days
We all can find fault and done something more
If we could take what we know now back to before
As we finish the story right up to today
We know in our heart what we wish to say
Each one of our thoughts different and unique
Just as the differences in each ones physique
The one thing in common that keeps us all bound
We're here at this moment this I have found
The book we have written is over and done
It's all of our past not forgotten but gone
At this very moment we all sit with pen in hand
A blank piece of paper, now we lead the band
No matter how empty or full our last book
We all have this moment to change our outlook
The book of your future starts this very minute
It's all up to you what will you put in it
The pages ahead are all white and pure
Much thought into every word, this I am sure
If you know love then I believe you are ready
If you don't then I suggest you remain steady
I think God is love is a good place to start

Just believe at all times with all of your heart
When you get to a point, you believe in the word
You'll be ready to fly as high as a bird
The book of your future good words start to flow
Words of a life that someone should know
I tell you don't waste one second of time
Every one wasted, there is no greater crime
So lets all begin with the flow of the pen
Our future at this moment is without any sin
I will tell you right now as for me and mine
I only plan a future for them so Divine
There is only one thing that I will always know
Wherever Jesus leads that's where I choose to go

THE THREE WISEMEN

Listen to the story I'm about to tell
Believe me when I tell you I know them all well
All were drawn to a bright shining star
Shining so bright it could be seen from afar
All led to the light by three beautiful daughters
Shining with their own love that never falters
The men were wise and worthy way back then
The only reason they were ever invited in
Once inside their wisdom it grew
Love and understanding they now knew
Wise to notice their life
Wise to make them their wife
Wise to want to stay near
Wise to still be here
I am one, two my brother-in-law
We grew wiser, they led us to him through Ma.

Eyes of a Child

Every time I look into the eyes of a child
I see what they see and I think it is wild
They tell me a story without saying a word
Every single emotion of which I've ever heard
Maybe love and happiness or sorrow and shame
A simple need for someone to know their name
Fear and embarrassment even pride and real heart ache
How can anyone miss all that is at stake?
If you wonder how good their life has been
Just kneel down and ask their story will begin
Often surprised wonder why you would care
As they play with you their thoughts they will share
I recommend you try it, I never miss the chance
Listen to their stories their mind sure can dance
Adults took the time taught me to love and give
But kids remind me how we all need to live
Some don't take time to just sit and be a kid
Every time I missed out I wished I never did
Playing with the young keeps you in your youth
I have no doubt that what I speak is the truth
I know God is smiling when he looks down and sees
Adults in the floor playing on their knees
Thank God for showing me things I would have missed
Playing catch, hide and seek even teddy bears I've kissed
A tea party for me or go catch lightning bugs
You've touched their heart when they run give you hugs
So many ways blessed all I ever have wanted
Nothing means more than the grasshoppers we hunted
Brighten their days is what we all need to do
Not just for them, but to find the child lost in you

Children are the future for us all. They will run the last days of our lives as we become less and less capable taking care of ourselves. It is important for each one of us to lead by example and lead them to the best understanding of their own abilities. After all, they most likely will be the ones to come to your rescue in your time of need. Every adult has the power and ability to build strong and confident young adults. If we fail them in any aspect of leading them to a brighter future, then we have failed ourselves and have left nothing of value here when we reach our destiny.

FOR THE BIRDS

Imagine the birds flying high in the sky
Wonder what they think as they fly by
Looking down at us and the changes we've made
As their world below turns a different shade
Once lush and green now a concrete gray
I wonder if they too can feel the dismay
Do they miss the place where they learned to fly
Do they pass by us now wondering why
The changes they see where made by mankind
I think we should stop maybe even rewind
Take down that old building, replant that old lot
Back to the way God originally thought
His greatest creation he handed to man
Ability and understanding to carry out his plan
We've gotten off track somewhere along the way
I think maybe it was when the birds flew away
They look for a place God left for them too
Not just a place made just for me and you
We can alter some choices and get back on track
We will know when we have when the birds all fly back

THE LIGHT IS NOT BLACK OR WHITE

When you read the title would you be one to believe
This is all about race nothing else to perceive
Thinking in black or white can show little vision
Accepting only one side with an important decision
I'm not writing this about the color of skin
It's more about the beliefs we all hold within
I don't understand when we are on the same ride
Seems oppositions everywhere pushed to pick a side
How did we make everything some big conflict
Only God holds the answers has the power to predict
Where are we headed with our one sided views
How did they become the only thing to make news
I bet he feels pain when he looks down at this mess
I'm not saying I know that one I can only guess
I know through his words his intentions were love
It's his sole purpose why he was sent from above
Consider his thoughts of love and all that they mean
Acceptance and forgiveness from you should be seen
My personal opinion most times kept to me
Demanding it be another's how wrong would I be
Ours is not to sit in judgment of any brothers
When they are not bringing harm to any others
What gives one the right to enforce an opinion on me
Just as wrong if I do it back to you don't you see
I won't go on you should know I'm no preacher
But someone is watching and that makes us all a teacher
That makes it important we all get it right
So the young can grow up and fight the good fight
There are so many answers still waiting out there
Are we so sure we know without looking everywhere
What's best for one may not be for another
God's children are different just ask every mother

That's the whole point all part of the plan
Tiny differences in us all every woman and man
He tells every life to choose their own path
All lead back to him without fear of his wrath
Forgiveness and love, acceptance and truth
Open mind and heart from the old to the youth
To all their free will within his guidelines
Somewhere in the middle it's compromise that defines
You see and hear with your heart, soul and mind
Impose your views on another and I bet you will find
God's not been with you as much as you think
If not in line with his words your demands stink
The very reason so no man would be oppressed
So why is control of another are so many obsessed
Remember, saying to others you must think like me
Just a pretender of God is all we will see
So before you dig in and prepare for a fight
Declaring your word from morning until night
Fight only for God and don't dare loose sight
He makes light in all colors not just black or white

33

FOREVER AND FOREVER

Forever and forever
I bet that you never
Heard words quite so clever
Don't use them to sever
To show you that whenever
The mind works like a lever
Use it well however
I wonder if you ever

Are you an achiever
Create one more believer
Words can be a cleaver
Take care for the receiver
Precision of the basket weaver
Constructive like the beaver
Don't be the deceiver
Don't be another leaver

Your words should help deliver
Their meanings make you shiver
It's best to be a giver
Give more than just a sliver
So take me to the river
It's more than chicken liver
The power to make you quiver
Best to be the great forgiver

Only good roads be a paver
For another be a saver
Don't leave one soul to be a craver
Let the truth never waiver
Don't be a backseat driver
You can be a holy diver
Don't you dare be a conniver
Even worse to be a depriver

Just show the world you're a lover
And the angels they will hover
Don't keep it under cover
Or you may not recover
Find your four-leaf clover
On the wings of a plover
This song is never over
Go back and start with forever

Forever and forever
Forever and forever
Forever and forever
Forever and forever
Forever and forever
Forever and forever
Forever and forever
Forever and forever

LIFE'S TROPHIES

Let me share with you this thought my friend
About how we use the time we spend
We choose a life and plan our course
Fly down our path like an untamed horse
Put all our efforts into obtaining our goal
Then realize from our own life we have stole
All of our efforts, every drop of sweat
What is it we seek or hope to get
A title, a trophy, riches and more
We work and struggle until our muscles are sore
We get to the end of the road we have taken
Now our beliefs ourselves we have shaken
It wasn't the glory the wealth or the fame
The best things in life all have a name
A parent, a coach, a friend or a teacher
Affecting our life like a really good preacher
There is nothing wrong with the goals that we seek
As long as our vision's not clouded or weak
Accomplishments we boast and hang on our wall
They all collect dust if their big or their small
Trophies aren't metal, have no monetary value
They're people on your path that reached out to help you
No rhyme or reason, they had nothing to gain
They helped with the goals you chose to obtain
If you sit where you are and fail to see this
I'm sorry to tell you the point you did miss
God, family and friends it all came through others
Our son's and our daughter's, our sister's and brother's
Do you give credit where credit is due?
And one more question I will ask of you
All of the lives you met on the way
How many, if any, you're a trophy they would say?

MOTHS TO A LIGHT

Our guardian angels hover around us like moths to a light. That's why it is so important to let love shine on others to make our light shine as brightly as possible. The brighter we shine the warmer the wings of our angels and the higher they fly just like moths to the light

LIFE SONG

We think we know the lyrics to someone else's song
When even with our own we can only sing along
Our life song slowly written with the people that we meet
Sometimes to influence us towards a different beat
We will change our words time and time again
As we live and grow making changes from within
Our lyrics make our song one of love or hate
Be sure to get them right before it becomes too late
If the song is right just like the message in your word
Up through the heavens your song will be heard
Sing everyday and remember this one thing
The last day of your life your song the angels sing

Short Quotes

Find God before he finds you somewhere you don't want to be.

Before I learned how to look I didn't see him in anything. Learning how to look, I now see him in everything.

He is always waiting for you. It's up to you to make the call.

You will find your perfect path will still lead you to times of imperfection.

You can't find him? Where are you looking?

I was lost and then I was found. Then I was told to go out and find others.

You don't have to look for love when it is all around you. Maybe you just need to stop discouraging it.

If you see the light, reflect it!

It's not our words that heal others. It's not others words that heal us. They are all His words.

Maybe you don't always have to look up to see God. It's possible to not see God while we knock Him out of our way, or we trip over Him as He lies before us.

These come too easy, I'm not that smart. That is how I know he puts the thoughts in my heart and mind.

Intelligence as well as the ability to have it all comes through Him too.

If you think your ideas mean more to more people than His do, I would love to bet you they don't.

How do I know anger doesn't come to us through God? People that are always angry have never even met Him.

God's love, heart, mind, eyes, ears, hands and feet in are every child. How did you come to be this way as an adult?

You'll never get the picture without taking the lens cap off.

What do I fear most since I found God? Nothing!

Keep talking, you're proving my point!

How can you feel abandoned when you left on your own kicking and screaming?

God knew I needed to find him before I found you. I was going to need all his gifts to deal with your mess.

God made chickens, pigs, turkeys, snakes, buzzards, bunnies, monkeys, apes, crabs, sharks, mules, pests, rats and mice. Along with all those people, he made good ones too.

If the truth frightens you then I would bet just about anything you are not very proud of yours.

If you think these are bad you should see the ones I came up with without Him.

Here's something I have come to know. People who see the good usually are. People who see the bad usually are. People who see it all screwed up usually are. People who only see problems usually are one. People who see love usually do. Starting to figure it out?

One way you can always recognize a true son or daughter of God is the resemblance.

I don't understand when so much can be seen in the light why someone would choose to sit in the dark.

These aren't prophetic or poetic; they are just reminders of Gods simple words.

Men have told me God was in them and I should follow them. Sometimes it is buried deep but I see God in all of us. That is why I follow God!

You didn't fall from his grace. You jumped!

This very second you should stop. See if you feel his presence. If not, keep waiting and look around.

There are people who actually feel sorry for me for believing these things. I sure feel sorry for them.

You're not lost? Then what's the problem?

The more I believe the more it works for me. You should try it.

How many times, just like me, did you think you knew? Only later to find out you didn't.

Blisters on my fingers, red tired eyes, hungry, mind slowing down and thoughts taking longer. I need to take a break but he said no.

How much can I write about Him? I don't know and never really will but He does.

I know people will belittle this. That is how WE know who THEY are.

You don't need a second opinion when you have God's.

Maybe you had more chances at happiness than others. Maybe you missed them or ran them off complaining that they never came.

Happiness is a choice! Get up and have some!

You will start hearing from God when you stop listening to the Devil.

Take time for your kids or regret it.

How many times did the one that walked away go nowhere?

If you can't find any value in these words don't complain to me. He speaks and I write.

When it comes to mankind God prepared a feast. That doesn't mean every man will taste it.

You can make your life a lot better any time you choose too. Just go out and make someone else's life better and watch what happens.

He loves even when you can't understand why.

How does it work? Go out and love then love some more. If nothing happens go out and love some more. Don't stop and when you have replaced some of the love you have stolen in the past he will start sending it back to you.

Happiness is just a state of mind anyone can enjoy if they choose to do so.

My Proudest Moment

The past few years I have found myself asking people what makes them proud and brings joy into their life. You get all kinds of answers from love, kids, jobs, little things, success, money and many more. I don't know why, but I enjoy listening to the different answers. I even try to get them to explain how they think they came to feel that way. As someone who has been blessed in very many ways, I am constantly looking back on my life to see how everything came together for me. The answers always amaze me as well as the thoughts of what those things mean to each individual. In some ways I have felt guilty at times for having so many opportunities and blessings when I listen to the stories of lives that weren't so blessed. I have even had a few go as far as to say they didn't really have a moment that stood out in their mind making them feel proud. How sad is that?

Every time I think back on the events that gave me a sense of pride there is one that sticks out in my mind as special. It always makes me smile and feel good about myself. It means so much to me that my wife has listened to the story several times. She would be the first to say that it affected me in many ways, and I have spent most of my time trying to repeat the experience. I think what intrigues me the most is how small it seems compared to other things I have done in my life. On the other hand it may be one of the most powerful things I have ever done to affect someone else for the better.

My daughter decided to sign up for little league when she was four years old. My wife decided to sign me up as coach so when they returned from registration I found out my latest responsibility. I had played ball but never anything like this. I remember being a little apprehensive about it at the time. Actually, I thought it would be a bad experience. It was not something I was looking forward to. I had no clue at that time how big a part of our life it would become or how much we all would enjoy it. It ended up being ten years of my life I wouldn't trade for anything.

Every year, eleven to fifteen girls came together in an attempt to create a ball team. Because my daughter was one of these girls, I was able to increase the time I got to spend with her. I don't think anyone will ever truly know how many hours we spent at practice, games or just in the back yard playing catch. It was a wonderful time in our lives together. We will always look back on those days fondly with a smile.

Every year we had different players on our team. Some had natural talent that stood out at a very early age. It is so obvious how different we all really are when it comes to the different talents we are blessed with. There were always ones that had played before and those that were playing for the first time. It was always a challenge because each player had different abilities needed different levels of instruction. While teaching one how to bunt you found yourself teaching another which way to run around the bases. That was probably one of the things that kept it new and interesting to me. Everybody wants to be a winner and wants to have something they stand out at. Everyone, no matter how good they perceive themselves to be, has weaknesses and strengths in different areas. Some see their weaknesses and work hard to improve them. Some see their weaknesses and try to avoid those situations so they don't have to feel unworthy. Through the years as a coach I have seen those fears and weaknesses stand in the way of not only succeeding but even being willing to attempt the things they fear. It didn't only affect the way they played ball but it affected the way they looked at things. It affected the way they made friends and built confidence in themselves, which is what the whole program is all about. I've actually seen so called adults try to sweep some of these kids under the rug so they could win and they wouldn't have to be bothered with the extra work they needed. After all, players like that can cost the team a victory. How far off track does one have to be to adopt that theory? Anytime you see a child begin to retreat inside themselves, dealing with them properly becomes a very serious issue. For them it could affect the rest of their life. When an adult points out these inabilities without offering real help the problem often escalates into bigger issues.

When my daughter was eight or nine years old we had a girl on our team who was afraid to bat. Just the very thought of it would bring a look of terror upon her face. Even in the dugout just preparing to bat, you could see her demeanor change from happy to fear. Her fear went beyond normal. She wasn't just afraid. She had a look on her face of shear terror and it truly was hard to watch, especially for someone who has always enjoyed watching kids have fun. Once she was in the batters box it seemed time stood still for her. She seemed to freeze with fear. She wouldn't speak.

I don't even know if she could at that time, her fear was so strong. At that age in the game the coaches pitched and it was very hard to look into her eyes so afraid. It didn't matter how much I encouraged her. She would remain frozen every time. She wasn't waiting for a good pitch. She was just waiting for it to be over. She never swung the bat. All the encouragement in the world didn't help. We tried everything we could think of to get her to relax but it seemed as if everything failed. With little time to practice before the season it was obvious to me, the other players and parents that this was going to be an issue.

After the first few practices we did have moments of breakthrough were she did swing the bat. One or two failed attempts would just make her freeze up again. Our first game came and despite all the encouragement she never swung the bat the whole game. "One, two, three you're out! One, two, three, you're out again!" Not only was the whole experience devastating to her, it was hard to watch. Even the other team was rooting for the poor girl who wouldn't swing. It seemed the more we all tried to help her the more it added to her strife. I know we had some players that needed extra help, but this was the most difficult situation I had ever dealt with. It became quite evident through comments that were made, some weren't as forgiving and understanding as others. I knew we had to do something. Not so much for the team but for this frightened little girl who was now wanting to quit ball all together. We told her it was OK and we would see her next practice. To be quite honest I didn't know if we would see her again because I knew the whole experience had been very traumatic for her. I told my wife and daughter on the way home if she did show up at the next practice we were all going to have to try and help her.

I think what disappointed me most were the ones that came to me acting as if she should be left on the bench as much as possible. It was suggested to me to stick her way out in the outfield when I did have to put her in. There is no doubt in my mind this may have helped the team but it wasn't going to do anything for her except make the situation worse. It warmed my heart how many felt the same way I did. The real goal at hand was to help her find her confidence.

Next practice I was glad to see she was there. She still looked unsure of herself, but she looked a lot better than the last time I had seen her. I think I approached her situation more like a parent then a coach. I didn't want to single her out. Two other girls had struggled a little with their batting also. I decided this practice we would separate ourselves from the rest of the team so we could devote our time helping her. The other two coaches worked the rest of the team while the four of us worked on batting.

I rotated the three girls. While one batted the other two helped me field balls. When it came her turn as usual she told me she couldn't do it without even trying. I know I have mentioned before how that goes through me. I walked up to about ten feet from her and started tossing the ball real softly her direction. Once again, she was refusing to swing. After about ten pitches I finally got her to promise me she would swing the bat. I kept talking to her and asking her questions trying to distract her from her fear. Once she started swinging it became a matter of me bouncing the ball off the bat. I will never forget her face the first time the ball actually bounced off the bat. It was one of surprise and disbelief. I told her I knew she could do it the whole time. For the first time, I saw her actually looking forward to trying again. It didn't matter if she was swinging at the ball or I was just bouncing it off the bat, she was making a connection. Every time she hit the ball she smiled a little bigger and a little longer. I think I was smiling bigger and longer every time too. Standing so close to her, I took a couple of pretty good shots from the hit balls but it was all well worth the bruises.

Without even noticing, I was stepping back farther and farther the whole time. Eventually I had to bring it to her attention that I was standing all the way back where I was supposed to pitch from. After about an hour all three were starting to hit the ball more consistently than before. All of them were building more confidence in their abilities. It was even starting to get where they were trying to outdo each other. I was very impressed with the progress all three made. I was extremely impressed with the progress being made by my new little friend. I was helping her and she could see the progress she was making. Her whole demeanor and attitude was changing right before my eyes. At that time I still had no way of knowing how much this evening was going to mean to both of us.

We took turns batting for the remainder of practice, and that was all it took to witness a total transformation in that little girl. Not only was she not afraid to bat, she was actually eager to get the chance to try again. It was starting to get late, so we called all the girls together and discussed what time to show up for the next game. We had a short little meeting on the infield and told them all we would see them the next day. The whole time this little girl who had come to us so timid and shy was boasting to the other girls how many times she had hit the ball. I remember feeling a sense of accomplishment while I was standing there watching her boast to the other girls. Some of the other parents who had stayed to watch practice were also impressed with what they had just witnessed. We all were amazed at the difference in her attitude and effort. Everyone who commented had felt just as bad as we had watching her struggle with her fears.

I will never forget what two hours of time and understanding did for her. The person I was looking at now was not that same little girl we had felt so sorry for. Not only was she now willing to try, she was looking forward to it. Most of the girls had left and we were hanging around waiting on a couple of parents to arrive. My wife and I were talking to a couple of other parents when her mom pulled up. Almost immediately the little girl started calling my name and asking if she could show her mom. I was more than glad to help her show off her new talent to her mom. We got out the equipment and she ran up to the batters box. Her mom was already in shock just at the fact she wanted to bat. Pitch after pitch she drove out into the grass with one of the biggest smiles on her face that you can imagine. She didn't want to stop. After every pitch she would say, "Throw me another one!" For several minutes we stood out there watching her do her thing. Everyone still at the diamond was enjoying watching her joy. Eventually it got dark outside and it became too hard to see. I had to put an end to all the fun before someone got hurt. As we put the gear up for the second time her mom approached me and thanked me for the unbelievable transformation she saw in her daughter. I could see the sincerity in her eyes, and I can't explain in words how good they made me feel inside. Eventually everything was loaded back up and we all went home.

All that night all I could think about was that little girl and how much she had changed in such a little amount of time. I couldn't stop smiling about it. I couldn't stop thinking about it. Seeing what a little time and effort could do to change someone's life really touched me in a way like nothing else I have ever done. I couldn't stop thinking about how little we have to do to make a real difference for someone else. The feeling I got from it was so powerful and rewarding that all I could think about was doing it more often. The whole situation had moved me so much I couldn't sleep that night, because I couldn't stop thinking about it. I remember being proud of my family for being the type of people to take that time. I was proud of the way my daughter went out of her way to make her feel included.

The next couple of games she struggled still, but she went down swinging. She was disappointed, but the rest of us were very proud of her. I think she was trying too hard to show what she could do. The best part of this story is that this same little girl became one of our best hitters by the end of season. We could actually count on her to make a difference when we needed it. She was making new friends and had really come out of her shell. I had several people come to me and comment on her progress. She was quickly becoming one of my greatest success stories. None of us knew everything going on with her, but we all knew she had made a complete turn around.

Toward the end of the season her mom approached me to thank me again. She began to explain to me how she and her husband were going through a divorce and it had been very hard on her daughter. It had been affecting her schoolwork and her ability to make friends at school. I learned that the girl had been steadily getting worse, and her mom was getting worried about how much everything had been affecting her. She told me she didn't know what to do. The very reason they had signed her up for ball was to try something new and hope she made some new friends. She said she couldn't thank me enough, and I told her she didn't have to.

We finished out the rest of the season, and, as always, I found it hard to say goodbye to all the girls and their parents. You become good friends with a lot of those people throughout the summer. In some ways you become co-parents with everyone, looking out for each other just like a family. In ten years time we made ten new families and enjoyed almost all of them. After all the gear was turned in and thoughts had moved on to other interests, we often took time to reflect on it all. We knew we had made a difference in that little girl's life, but we had no idea how much.

I run into parents and girls from those years all the time, and it is always nice to see them. But I soon noticed that every time we ran into that one girl she was hanging out with girls from that team. She had made some of her best friends that summer. I don't think her life would be the same it is today if we wouldn't have helped her feel like she fit in. Even more remarkable to me is how she looks at the three of us. She stops by still to this day just to say hello to my wife and I. My daughter is eighteen now, along with most of the girls we played ball with, and I still see her with the friends she made that summer. I started realizing just how much more there was to those summer teams than hitting a ball. The things that were being learned go a lot farther than just out on the ball field. We really are teaching things that will affect those kids the rest of their life.

I know I will never forget the little girl who came to us scared to swing and left with everyone referring to her as slugger. I think of her all the time. I use it to remind myself that we all can make a difference. I use it to make myself feel better when I face issues that seem to be too much to deal with it. Can and can't are two very powerful words. Depending on which one we are most familiar with in our life we determine our own abilities. I think all too often we sell ourselves short. I have learned over the years we all fail to recognize and reach our full potential. Sometimes we learn of abilities we didn't know we had when a situation arises that tests all we have inside. How many times are we forced to react to something, and then we look back and say, "I didn't know I could do that!"

All I know for sure is still to this day, when I look back on my life, that girl's story always comes to mind as one of my greatest accomplishments. Whenever the conversations turn to things that make us proud come up, I think of that terrified little girl who wouldn't swing. The only reason I can come up with for that to be my proudest moment is the fact that most of the things that had made me proud were things that made my life better. This was something I knew had made a major difference in someone else's life. I have seen kids like that before who would rather quit than face their fears. I have seen kids like that who weren't handled properly and the situation actually got worse. Often we get those types of opportunities and fail to get it right. This time I knew we had got it right and actually made a difference that lasted. I know I have never witnessed such a change in someone before in such a short period of time. I sit here today looking back and seeing the results with a new thought about the whole thing. I know without a doubt that little girl taught me a lot more than I did her. I will always be grateful and never forget the valuable lesson I learned about how important it is to take a little extra time for those who need it. I promise, you will never find anything more rewarding. I know in almost fifty years of life I haven't. I strongly recommend that if the opportunity ever comes to you to take the time to make a difference in someone's life, you should take it. You will get so much out of it, and you will find yourself going out and looking for those opportunities.

Who I AM

As a baby I was born in the year 1963
Seven years in town the rest in the country
That's where I learned to hunt, fish and live
A solid foundation my parents still give
Straight A's came easy all through school
Maybe not a genius, certainly no fool
When it came to athletics I did it all
There was base, basket and foot ball
I've been a pitcher, captain and quarterback
At 18 years experiences few did I lack
Right out of high school I married my wife
Together we began our brand new life
A son and a daughter I love them so much
So many ways my heart they did touch
27 years construction my profession
Working with my dad taught me dedication
My grandfather loved God, very active in church
Shoveled steps, stoked the fire, played the organ in search
To please God so important that's what I was told
Don't be ashamed instead proud and bold
I think that's the reason I've always been blessed
Answers seem to come, seems like we never guessed
Use all he gave us to the best of our ability
Good or bad situations never seek any pity
Without God our own businesses we couldn't start
We run them like our life guided by the heart
Constant opportunities bless our whole family
God is the reason we live so happily
We both know it was him who sent our kids to us
I think of that all the time to keep from throwing a fuss
More grateful I have grown the older I get
Not just for my life but for all there's a net

We've always known you watch over every minute
Even when I had to look hard to find you in it
We experienced a miscarriage why we didn't know
And when she lost her father almost a fatal blow
The worst she lost her mother just the other day
I know you heard me for her and Ma I did pray
Thirty years of marriage marked in stone this year
Thinking back ten years I can't believe we're still here
Twenty years of possessions all went up in the fire
All possessions were lost, trust that I'm no liar
Nothing we were left but the clothes on our back
We could put all of our belongings in a paper sack
God, family and friends even the Red Cross
I can't list them all those who helped with our loss
A wave of God's children sent support our way
My whole family grateful still to this day
Another ten years our life filled with God's favor
All who helped us it's their kind hearts I savor
Our love of people returned to us down and out
From beginning to end God's work I have no doubt
This year will mark our thirtieth anniversary
A countless number of friends hardly one adversary
I can't imagine my life without all those bridges
Thankful they weren't burned to face doors without hinges
Now more than ever we see someone in need
Do all we can to help plant a new seed
We're not looking for credit it's truly not ours
Credit goes to God way out past the stars
When I take a look at every kind act of mankind
I see it all comes from God that's what I find
When people ask me I say I'm just one simple man
Who see's God everywhere with him I know I can
So many unbelievers who say you're just a scam
But I see clear your love made me who I am

THE WATERFOWLER'S SOUL

Imagine a four year old child
His father and him out in the wild
In the dark before the sunrise
Waiting on it with eager eyes
Calls in the night most would fear
Calm and collected his hero is here
The colors fade in along with the light
Witness the passing gone is the night
Cold winter morning, we welcome the sun
Lighting all beauty and the works he has done
Learning so much such a young boy
Being led to the truth a real natural joy
The story goes he was led by the father
How many take the time or would even bother
Taught true respect for all that's created
Information we need it's never out dated
All creatures are beautiful and I think that's how
I found so much enjoyment through waterfowl
A big part of my life nearly fifty years old
I still look forward to stepping out in the cold
I was that young boy way back in the start
Memories from back then still fill my heart
There are beautiful colors found in the feathers
Ways to find shelter in all kinds of weathers
How much joy is found in the time that is spent
In God's house so much that's why we went
I never stepped out into God's home
Without feeling him there every step I roam
God, dad and I share a love for those birds
He gave them beauty their special in his words
He said to let the fowl fill the skies
I think of him when I look in their eyes

How does a man explain the depths of his soul
Things to fill your glass or to the rim of your bowl
God and my dad, the fowl and I have a bond
Everyday it means more and I grow so fond
Work hand in hand to keep his work alive
So man, beast and fowl can all start to thrive
Without working for all it works for none
From God to the father now passed to the son
Check in with the fowl as long as they're doing well
His work carried out what a story to tell
When I get a call I look up to heaven
Fowl checking on me a message he's given
All I can think what a beautiful sight
A bond made at four years still held onto tight

THE RIVER

Let me tell a little story
Where I found my road to glory
It's where I go in a hurry
I need an answer to a worry
It's where I've always found
His gifts for us abound
I can see it all around
I can hear every sound
I'm not seeking any fame
Search for answers why I came
Where I go to call His name
Every time it's been the same
His answers seem to come to me
A brighter picture my eyes see
It's the place I feel most free
A very sacred place to be
The muddy water flowing by
I look up and see the sky
Many times I asked him why
Find the strength for my best try
Seems his words pop in my head
Without a word being said
Knowledge unlike books I've read
I will return until I'm dead
In the church that He created
A place you can feel elated
Before my wife and I had dated
I knew this place was underrated
Means so much to me today
Barely find the words to say
It's where we go to play
Drop to our knees and pray

When you sit down by the water
Step away from the slaughter
Come to know your son and daughter
Feel the touch of the master potter
Molding us so we can feel
Where he began to reveal
Stay in touch with all that's real
The first place we sealed the deal
When you listen to the breeze
Rustling through the trees
Your thoughts will start to ease
These are the moments you should seize
In God's house is where you are
Learning this will take you far
For us shines every star
Might hear the strum of his guitar
Listen close the angels sing
All around they're taking wing
Wisdom all his creatures bring
The place I learned most everything
So many things he wants to show
How all life moves with the flow
Things he needs us all to know
The only way for us to grow
Easy to see he was a giver
Knowing his words will make you shiver
He's never failed to deliver
When I knelt down by the river

THE EULOGY

How would you react today, if a loved one passed away
And members of the family asked if you would stand and say
Words of love to honor a life that's here no more
When everyone who knew them never felt heartache so sore
Knowing there are no words, no actions you can take
Express the greatness of their life get it right for heaven's sake
At first I felt unworthy too great a task for me
Describe a life as seen by all not just what I did see
Doubt replaced by honor it seemed no time at all
Grateful for the chance to speak and glad I got the call
I never took so seriously a task that lay before
It was hard to find the words with my heart so tore
Up all night just to write good thoughts filled my head
Select very carefully all the things that should be said
I wrote three different versions all were filled with love
Took my time with every line for help I looked above
The time came and I could not decide which one to use
Wouldn't matter all were nice but one I had to choose
I can't believe how calm I felt like I was on a mission
When I asked what I should do he sent me a vision
Ma was standing at his side he said with me they'd stand
And if I felt I needed help I could hold their hand
When I stood up I knew that I had made a choice
I didn't choose the written word I used my mind and voice
Words of love came easy just speaking from the heart
When we speak of such great love there is no stop or start
I'll never forget the faces of family and friends
The teary eyes, the mournful cries, of love that never ends
Without a pause, without breaking down I tried to do my best
Tell you my friend never before my faith put to the test

The words that passed through me heart felt is all I know
I think Ma left me one last gift before she had to go
The task was spiritual in itself along with her goodbye
It's stayed with me everyday I think I might know why
In some ways she stayed with me I can feel her deep inside
I think that a part of me left with her on that final ride
Don't pass the chance if offered you sometime
To honor someone in such a way truly is sublime
Standing with God and angels, loved ones already gone
Something will change inside of you like the light of dawn
I know I'll always wonder if my words were right
I won't know until my time and I sit down that first night
Back down at Ma's table where I'll look her in the eye
I know what her words will be and I know just why
It's what she said every time when her heart I did touch
They would be "that's my boy" words to me that mean so much

REFLECTION

Everything in our life good or bad
Have one thing in common happy or sad
Things that take you in a different direction
You can or you can't make the connection
Right and wrong are found in the truth
The adult today formed as a youth
The one who can make life rich or poor
Someone who cares or care not anymore
You might find someone full of insight
Or someone who fails, fall short of right
Everything capable of being reversed
Not always easy life can't be rehearsed
What you find might make you smile
Power to change inside you all the while
It could be the eyes of a child
Easy to see, tender and mild
It will often take a second look
Not seeing all first glances took
Look at the one who stands before you
If all you could change, what would you do
I promise today you will never see clearer
Take a long look when you look in the mirror

SHORT QUOTES

What do you want on your back: monkeys or wings?

He blessed you with looks. Do you use them for His benefit or yours?

I know you can, but I wouldn't (live without God).

I know you won't, but I will (live with God).

God made the ass, but Jack made himself one.

Before listening to you, I couldn't understand how you could think you know more than Him. After listening to you speak, I'm starting to figure it out.

Man has a tendency to use everything he can to meet his needs.

You know who is most grateful for planes, trains and automobiles? The horse!

OK, I won't call you selfish. I'll just call you someone who is never happy unless you get your way.

Be kind you might still get what you want. Keep complaining and I bet you don't.

I see only brothers and sisters, even the ones that maybe should be kept in the closet.

I don't know what all these mean, but when I read them back they don't sound like me, they sound more like Him

I can't do this by myself. Ask my wife!

Some people won't believe until pigs fly. I saw one loaded on a cargo plane today.

You may live your whole life in denial then wake up one day in agreement with Him. Looking back, you see you couldn't make yourself; you will see how he made you.

I don't read a lot. I write even less. I spend my time doing what some only read about. For some reason this matters to me.

It's impossible to believe, succeed, live, love, find, learn, see, hear, smell, touch or understand any of these without all his blessings

We must blame ourselves when we end up in the dark. We knew better than to go there.

You may think you know how much he loves but I'll bet it's more than you can even imagine

Hope for the hopeless, path for the lost, light for the dark, food for the hungry, love for the lonely, strength for the weak, sight for the blind, sound for the deaf, shelter for the homeless, thoughts for the mind . . . Should I go on, or are you starting to get it?

You might think all are lost in a bar. I've seen just as many lost in a church.

God stands for you so why don't you?

If someone asked me where to find God you might be surprised at my answer: not in a book, not a man, not a religion, not a cloth, not a steeple, not a sign or a mind. I would suggest you look in your heart. He's in there you just covered him up with the trash you keep in there.

Stomping and screaming for His thundering voice? Sit and be quiet, listen for a whisper.

Isn't it strange some have never met Him while others can introduce you to several different images of him?

One of His ways is most simple. What ever it is you wish to come into your life, just start giving it.

If you want to help the needy, buy this book!

Without a sense of humor you might as well have no sense at all.

Would it help if I told you every time you make someone smile an angel puts a star by your name?

If you choose to spend your time with people who are just like you then you aren't learning much are you?

This has been good for me. If you don't have God you are on your own.

I don't want people to believe because I do. I don't expect them to. I want and expect them to be smart enough to figure it out for themselves.

If I stop now look how much time will have been wasted

I can take you to God's house anytime you wish to go. It has one roof sometimes clear sometimes cloudy, the ceiling lights are the stars, the carpets are the lush green fields, the mountains his walls, the oceans his pool and everyone is welcome all day and night

Don't think I think I know everything. He teaches me everyday, and I still have a lot to learn.

You think you are too good, and I think that's what makes you not good enough.

Everyone goes around making noise. You just have to determine which end it is coming out of.

I told him I was getting writer's cramp, and He said he didn't want to hear it. His voice told me to keep writing.

If you think the Lord works in mysterious ways figure this one out. I asked him for a way to reach more people and he stuck me in this office alone at a desk.

God created too many beautiful things to list. He never created anything more beautiful for the eyes of man than a woman.

The sun rises, the rain quenches, the river flows, the grass grows, the wind blows, the cloud floats, the mountain peaks, the ocean waves, the fish swims, the animal lives, the bird flies, the tree shades, the leaf falls, the rainbow glows, the moon phases, the star shines, the planet rotates, and the universe expands. What do you do?

He created all this, and you can't make a sandwich?

Maybe they will refer to me as the misguided prophet.

He knows what you are doing. Do you?

You won't find piece of mind in a lazy body.

Guarding your heart to closely from what you don't want to get in may keep the things you do want to get in from being able to.

It's hard to fly as high as the angels on a pitchfork.

If you asked and he didn't answer, thank him!

You better hope it doesn't take as long to find your way back as it did to realize you were lost.

You said you didn't believe or need Him in your life, and, now that you are hanging over the edge, you ask Him to pull you back up. He will.

I'm not an in-your-face type of believer. I'm more of an in-your-heart believer.

He will take you back even when you know He shouldn't.

THE LITTLE MAN

My kids will tell you the one pet peeve that will get a response out of me faster than anything is "I can't". In our house that has always been completely unacceptable for an answer to anything. I was raised to never say "I can't" and I am very proud of what that has done for me in my life. We all know that is the best way, so why is the government, law, parents, teachers, coaches, preachers and other people in positions of power spending so much time telling everyone else, "they can't?" I want to know in my house and on my property what makes anyone think they have a right to tell me I can't do anything I choose. Because I will tell you right now, they don't. They can take their "can't" attitude and spend the rest of their days not being capable of anything; that's fine with me. Just remember, I'm quite capable of choosing for myself, thank you. I can do anything. The problem with those people who can't is they think no one else can or should. Now we are being forced to teach this way of thinking to our kids. Helmets, kneepads, elbow pads, too cold for the playground, don't keep score, everybody wins and how about slow down so everyone else can catch up. Why wouldn't we fall behind standing around waiting on the slow ones? We used to push people to stand out and they did. Now someone wants that to be a bad thing but no one wants to admit it. This goes beyond those few that just fear being alone and try to keep their little baby a little baby forever. This is more an attempt to make this whole country that little baby forever. I will never be able to adopt this new so-called "American way" to be my own because it goes against everything I know to be right. I believe the majority of people think the same way. It is only those with that hidden agenda of destroying this country and the freedom it stands for who agree with this new "you can't" attitude

Let me tell you a story about what I learned of the difference between "I can" and "I can't." The two words "I can't" where removed from my vocabulary by my grandfather when I was seven years old. He asked me if I would be interested in going to work with him all summer. I'm seven years old and just got offered my first job. I thought that was pretty cool, so I took it. I bet you will be surprised just what that job consisted of.

Grandpa worked on and managed his brother's cattle ranch. His brother also owned an implement company in Harrisburg where he spent most of his time in the office. If you think Grandpa was much of a baby sitter, you would be mistaken. Actually, Grandpa was a real cowboy. He spent his life on a horse. He made a good living on that horse too. He was one of the good cowboys. My grandpa was an Illinois State Trooper when there were only two from Effingham south. He was well over six-feet tall. He was one who definitely walked tall and carried a big stick. He was not one to put up with a lot of bull. I had no clue what I was in for that summer.

While my friends were riding bicycles, shooting baskets and playing catch, I was learning the value of a dollar, not to mention what it means to have a job and responsibilities. I had no idea how much that summer would effect the rest of my life. I'll never forget that first morning getting up at 5:00. I had toast for breakfast and was in the passenger seat by 5:30. It was a thirty-minute drive to Harrisburg and starting time was 6:00. Grandpa's brother met us at the farm that first morning so he could discuss my job and my pay before I went to work. He asked me if I had a horse. I told him I didn't. He told me I couldn't work on a cattle ranch without one. He pointed to about twenty horses in a pasture and asked me if I saw one I liked. I pointed to a sandy colored mare with a dark mane.

It makes me smile thinking back to him telling me, "That one is yours. I'll pay you two dollars a day, Payday is on Friday. Come down to the office with your grandpa and I will cut you a check."

I remember at that point thinking, *this job stuff is pretty cool*. I just showed up and already they are giving me all kinds of stuff.

After he left, Grandpa and I went out to get my new horse. We put a halter on it and led it back into the barn. The saddle I would need to ride was waiting in the barn, and that was when I got my first real lesson in the difference between "I can" and "I can't." I was told to saddle up and get ready to go check the cows and the fences. Without moving or attempting to do anything I said, "I can't". Thinking back I think I would have been better off to kick Grandpa in the shin.

"How do you know you can't," he said. "You haven't even tried! Don't tell me you can't. Now, get over there and saddle that horse," was all he had to say.

I carried the saddle over to the horse and looked up. I said, "I can't even reach his back." When I looked at grandpa I could tell I hadn't impressed him with my efforts.

"Well look around here there is always a way. What about one of those straw bales? It's your job. Do you think I'm going to do everything for you?"

Reluctantly I put down the saddle, walked over to a bale, and drug it over to my new horse. By that point I was starting to not like my new job so much. It was starting to turn into a lot of work. It took every bit of strength I had, but I got that saddle up there. I learned a valuable lesson from Grandpa that day. It was my first day and it hadn't even really started yet but I was already learning my abilities exceeded my own knowledge of them. I learned that instant what an "I can" attitude is capable of doing compared to an "I can't" one.

It didn't take long after we left the barn to realize I wasn't just along for the ride. There were things that needed to be done, and I was expected to be able to do them. Not one single day that summer was I treated like a kid or, even worse, a baby. Grandpa didn't soften it up for the delicate ears of a seven year old. He treated me and talked to me like any other hired hand. It wasn't, "Be careful little buddy. Don't get hurt trying to get across that ditch." It was more like, "Get over there and cut them off now. Hurry up you can do it." There wasn't time to think whether or not I could do it. I was doing it before I had time to think about the fact that I have never done anything like this before. I had been riding all my life. I was raised around horses. They tied me in the saddle and led me around when I was one year old.

The memories I have from that summer will stay with me as long as my memory does. I learned how to do many things that summer. Feeding livestock (horses, cows, pigs, chickens, dogs, etc.), herding cattle, cleaning equipment, mending fences, riding, roping, calving, branding, immunizations, ear tagging, castrating, hauling to market, auctions and anything else that pops up on a working ranch. I learned about each one day by day working side by side with Grandpa. I know how much a seven-year-old boy can grow towards becoming a man with the right guidance. Most people who are over protective can't even imagine allowing such a thing to even happen. Seems in today's world seven-year-olds aren't that capable anymore. From what I hear they can't do anything. The sad thing is most of them will be fifty and still assume they can't do anything. Do you know how many adults I've heard say they can't saddle a horse without even trying? It proves what I have said all along, that we don't realize our abilities and never reach our full potential, not because of others, but because of or own mind. We talk ourselves out of most of the things we are capable of by determining without any effort that we can't.

How many seven-year-olds can say they swam a creek on horseback then bolted up a wooded hillside and turned the whole herd singlehandedly. I'll bet not very many. I wonder how many have taken a herd down a busy city street while cars sit in the middle of the road watching cows brush down both sides of them and wave as you ride past? I remember watching Grandpa ride out in the middle of a mud bog, jump from his horse to tie a rope to a pregnant cow, and then drag her out before she gave birth in there. Once he had her out I helped the cow with the delivery. We would go home every evening with dirt, sweat, manure and no telling what else ground into our clothes. We would drive home smiling and laughing about what happened today. Then we would spend time talking about what was going to have to be done tomorrow. I remember stopping at a gas station on the way home to get a soda. Grandpa would have an RC and I would have a "White Lightning" cream soda. Forty years later, Grandpa is gone, his brother is gone, the old gas station is gone and even the old farm is gone. It was replaced with shopping centers, stoplights and subdivisions. I sure miss all that has been lost since then. Like I said, times sure do change. I think at seven-years-old I learned more about life, responsibility, jobs, money and believing in the things I can do instead of the things I can't than some do in a lifetime.

I will never forget going to the office the first Friday to pick up my check. I was a workingman. I had money. I took that check home and put it in my sock drawer. Ten dollars. I remember thinking at that time I was rich. Only later in life did I realize I was rich at that time, just not monetarily. In my mind I was a man. I was doing what men do. As far as I was concerned, if that was what made them men then that must be what it made me. It helped that people were making comments about me acting like a little man or working like a little man. I don't think anyone else could have taught me so much at such an early age. Anyone else would have tried to baby me and hold me back. My grandpa taught me I could do anything. Even things I had convinced myself I couldn't. He didn't do it by telling me, showing me or doing it for me. He let me show myself by putting trust and faith in my abilities. Talking to and treating me like a man went a long way towards making me one. I think it is easy to confuse the youth of today when we constantly tell them, "you can't do this and you can't do that." After we have convinced them they can't, then we tell them to start acting like adults. It's no wonder why so many teenagers are so confused today. I don't think a seven-year-old could be more confident in their abilities than I was.

I think I will always smile when I remember the first time we were working part of the farm closest to town. At lunchtime, when Grandpa asked me if I was ready to eat, he told me today we would have lunch in town. I was thinking we would go by truck, but his plan was to ride on into town on horseback. That's what we did. We road our horses up to the grocery store in downtown Harrisburg. Sadly, that old grocery store is no longer there either. We would tie our horses out front and go inside. Every time we went there grandpa would buy two cans of pork and beans, an RC cola and a "Yoo-Hoo" chocolate drink for me. He kept a can opener and plastic spoons on him. That would be our lunch, one or two times a week. Grandpa had many friends in there, and I could tell everyone was always glad to see him. I didn't speak much. I know I learned a lot just sitting there eating my lunch and listening to them talk. It would last about twenty minutes, and then we were out the front door back up on our horses. Experiences like that have an amazing effect on a seven-year-old boy. I wish every child could have the opportunity to think and do for themselves as I did that summer. Grandmas and grandpas have a lifetime of knowledge to share with the young. My life would have never been so fulfilling without the head start I had, especially compared to my friends who spent their summers playing games.

The strange thing about that summer was as it was enhancing my mind it was also creating a problem, through no fault of my grandpa or myself. It didn't matter what abilities he saw in me, the rest of the world still only saw a seven-year-old child. I found myself having to act younger than I felt to please the people who still thought I needed to be babied. I found it harder to relate to some of my friends because the things I learned seemed way more important to me than childish games. Very few adults are capable of looking at a seven-year-old child and seeing an adult. It is very understandable when I think about most of the seven-year-olds I knew and the ones I see today. I think that's one reason why I have always gotten along so well with kids. I don't look at them as children; I see them more as adults who just don't realize it yet. This experience even went so far as to show me the differences in parenting, and it explained a lot of the different results from those differences. It was quite some time before I realized how much grandpa had helped me tap into my abilities to do things thought by most to be impossible. Most people live their whole life without experiencing things that show them what I was shown at such an early age.

One lesson I learned that summer left a little bit of a bitter taste in my mouth. I wanted to buy a new bicycle with my money. Mom and Dad took me down to Western Auto so I could look at bikes and see if they had one I might be interested in. I hate to say that is another place of my past that no longer exists. Anyway, I found a metallic green three-speed bicycle that seemed to sit there and call my name. That was the one I wanted. I paid the man almost seventy dollars with tax and headed home with my new bike. Was I ever going to be so cool? I remember getting back home and unloading it like it was yesterday. It took me about thirty minutes to realize the hand brakes made it hard to lock them up and throw it sideways. I also learned that they didn't have all the bugs out of the multi-speed bicycles in 1970. It had to be one of the first bikes of its kind back then. Whatever problems I was finding with the bike didn't really matter because it was mine and I was stuck with it. I remember growing to hate that bicycle. At seven-years-old I had learned the hard way with my own money that outward appearances can be misleading. Shiny, new and expensive didn't necessarily mean better.

I was so fortunate to learn at such an early age that I can do things I never thought possible. That has stuck with me through out my whole life. I don't remember anything that came my way from that point on that I didn't feel capable of dealing with. It amazes me how little portions of our life can so greatly affect every other aspect of our life. When someone in our life that we see as capable in every way expresses the fact they see those same capabilities in you, it instills unbelievable confidence. I noticed with my new way of seeing things I had more confidence than some of the adults supposedly teaching me about life. It was hard from that point on to respect some of my elders when I saw things I could teach them, while they didn't see the need to listen. For several years after that I acted a lot younger than I felt just to keep the peace. Inside I felt like a man, but on the outside I was seen by the world as a little boy.

There is no doubt in my mind that this newfound confidence is what teachers and coaches noticed about me. That is the only thing that explains them coming to me and sending me to gifted classes or making me captain, quarterback, or pitcher. They went so far as to make examples out of me to others. The truth is, I wasn't gifted at all. I had just been given wisdom at an early age through my grandpa and what he saw in me that no one else did. He gave me a head start in life that should be offered to everyone. I often wonder just how much that summer did influence my life.

Now that I am a grandpa myself, I use what I learned at seven to teach my grandbaby who is just months old. It worked for both of our kids, and I know it will work for her also. I can't wait to watch her excel with the knowledge she is capable of more than she herself will ever even know. At ten months her advantages are already beginning to show. You can see her actually starting to realize this for herself. And that's exactly the way her life is going to stay. Learning and living for herself and making her own choices are using her own heart and mind as God intended. I've spent a lot of time since then raising, coaching, teaching and playing with kids, but only because I understand how important that time can be. Instead of showing kids what I can do, it has always brought me great joy allowing them to see for themselves what they can do. If you want to see true joy in a child's eyes, let them do it. No, they won't do it exactly right every time and yes there might be a little more of a mess to clean, but aren't those the moments in our life that really mean something? Or, am I the one missing the big picture?

I get very frustrated with what's going on in the world today. Everyone wants to take a stand and tell someone else what he or she can or cannot do. What a shame for so many to think they have that right. I strongly believe a lot of the laws on the books today exist because some man wanted his name in a law book. I also strongly believe many of these laws invade our constitutional rights to freedom of choice. Thank God my rights are protected under the constitution, which is under God not over him. Anything in the books today not coinciding with His Word is unconstitutional. Our forefathers were geniuses when it came to that one. The only way this country will ever get back on track is when our government gets back into good standing with God. If my name were on some of these new laws I would want it off because I know how offensive they are to His Words. I think if we get our country back to His Word we might see the wheels start turning in the right direction again.

Wouldn't it be nice if we could start tomorrow back to the basics of God's word and the constitution. God said you can. Shouldn't our government say you can? What if all our teachers and coaches said you can? At the very least, mom and dad must say you can if we are ever going to be able to fight the good battles that wait for us in the future.

It didn't have to be a cattle ranch. I could have learned just as much helping my other grandpa at church or helping Dad on the construction site. Where doesn't matter as much as who that time is spent with. A lot of moms are the person who teaches her children to fight the urge to cuddle and protect. I guess the closest thing I have been able to relate what I'm saying is by using the mama bird and her objective. She knows new ones will be coming every spring. She also knows time is limited for the young she has now. Her goal is not to keep them in the nest forever, but she tries to teach them all they can do for themselves in the little bit of time she has to do so. Her goal is to watch them fly for themselves. She spends everyday showing them they can do it. In just a few short months, just like that summer I spent with Grandpa, they are armed with all the information they need to live. Then she returns to start her purpose all over again. Are you one of those people keeping your baby birds from flying and becoming responsible adults? Keeping them from flying on their own out of fear of being alone can be such an injustice to the ones we say we love.

Bottom line is I am so grateful for that summer and all the amazing things it prepared me for. I will always be grateful for a grandpa that took the time to be bothered. I have vowed to spend the rest of my life helping others find that confidence and their own abilities. I think it is kind of a tribute to God and Grandpa. Nothing I have ever done in my life has ever brought me so much satisfaction. When I feel like I have made a difference, I sleep well at night and look forward to the next day. If you don't know me it would be easy to think I am just blowing smoke. The people who do know me will tell you that this is how I live every day of my life. It doesn't matter whether you are at home or at work, there are always opportunities to make a difference. I will always be grateful for that time I spent with Grandpa. I will never forget the summer I became a little man.

THE HEART

From the hand of God the first tiny beat
Pumping life into miniature hands and feet
Ticks like a timer, nine months in the oven
Into the world surrounded by lovin'
Stronger the beat with each passing day
The bigger it gets in the kid's as they play
Between child and adult we learn it can feel
Hold emotion inside that is very real
Some learn to young how much it can hurt
Hide it down deep or wear on the sleeve of your shirt
Early adults struggle with changing emotions
Rolling in and out like the waves of the oceans
The heart and the mind in some of us battle
Both of them strong we're harder to rattle
As an adult I know many have scars
While those in love will soar to the stars
We're taught how to feel with our fingers
To teach this of the heart nobody lingers
Our own heart teaches us about pain
In that no escape, we all try in vain
It lets us know what brings us joy
Hard to control broken hearts can destroy
From the first powerful pain in the heart
One quickly learns and guards it they start
Emotion and the heart a double-edged sword
No happy without sad, it can't be ignored
Love or hate, strong or weak, selfish or giving
One without the other there is no living
There is no escaping with those we most care
Their loss will bring the heart its deepest despair
The strength of the mind determines how much abuse
Before one hides within refusing to turn it loose

The ones we all know lost and alone
Refuse to go out or pick up the phone
Guarded so tightly that love can't get in
Help needed quick before depression can begin
Lucky in life if your hearts never there
It finds most of us all sometime, somewhere
It's not only blood the heart pumps and flows
Love in and out of it constantly goes
If you choose to live a long happy life
More feelings of love than feelings of strife
Here's something you may want to think about
For love to come in make room pump some out
The heart is amazing so much it can do
Until your last breath it beats the life into you

So A Child Understands

God spoke to me, some say that's absurd
I listened to him, this is what I heard
This project you work on and you wonder why
The words pop in your head seem to fall from the sky
I put them in you while living your life
Through family and friends, your kids and your wife
He said that He noticed I was paying attention
Then He told me He knew it was all good intention
Now the more that I write I feel He guides me
At the start I had questions even I couldn't see
I feel I'm quite smart, why use words so simple
Cute but falls short of a smile and a dimple
I picked up a pen the words started flowing
I just kept on writing without even knowing
I'm sitting up late, so I can write
Seems I can't stop night after night
Many ways He has spoken to all of us
Sometimes it gets missed, lost in the fuss
I felt so much better everyday that went by
It comes so easy I don't even try
The words I have lived that's how I know them
How I got here today writing this poem
I took pen and paper, sat down in my chair
Searching for words, the right ones to share
Every time I write now, answers come from the heavens
That's why my life seems to be rolling me sevens
Since the very first word I've written today
I asked then I listened and I heard Him say
When I speak to you without voice you might find
Words from my heart passed into your mind
He said I'm sending these words at this very time
Intentionally simple are these in this rhyme

They've scrambled my words like eggs in a skillet
Some go as far as to destroy and kill it
Don't boast with big words their meanings to seek
The simplest words will show strength not weak
I want all to know more than just one religion
It's not about wealth, there's more than one condition
I'm tired of all of the judgment and division
It's not the color of skin or a single man's vision
It's about thoughts and feelings we all keep within
The hearts and minds of all women and men
I choose not only to speak to philosophers and PhD's
Simple words will be heard without all the studies
My words will go farther they'll flow like the breeze
Just keep writing the ones you say come with ease
When I sent you these words the problem in all our hands
Is keep it simple enough a child understands

PASSING JUDGMENT

I think the most common way to fall from grace
At least what I see most in peoples face
It's judgment of another life we have all participated
Makes getting along with someone else so complicated
Ours not to judge that's what I read in his words
That means every finger we point is for the birds
How can one be of God and go against his rule
To think he sides with you, you must be a fool
Everywhere I go people do it in his name
Take his name in vain I think, would be the same
His intention everyone not to be just like you
What gives you the right, think you can tell me to
The more I listen the more I think most miss the point
Acceptance is the only way that we don't disappoint
If you talk behind another's back on any given day
I hope you know you need to stop and pray
I'll be the first to admit, difficult to say the least
I have failed more than once in the battle with the beast
Ones that seem to take on the roll of judge
Seems they walk around like they hold a grudge
Do you think they know they have turned away from God
They believe he is on their side, I find that quite odd
The one who judges others is afraid to judge himself
They think they're God's little helpers like Santa has an elf
Without our help how will God ever get through
Can't get into their life if he can't get in through you

This is for those who think they know much better
Do you follow his word right down to the letter
Do your words comfort those with which you disagree
Or do you save those for the ones who think like thee
You'll never find happiness if you don't learn to cope

People have different ideas how does that steal your hope
No surprise different minds might add something to yours
His plan brings us together so we can unlock the doors
To new ideas for mankind so we might get it right
Just remember that some will kick, scream and fight
In no way do we wish to be just like you
How's that for a thought on which you can chew
As for me I only wish to be more like him
He told me to be like you would make my chances slim
Of ever finding the good life he made for me
Judge not I do my best, that's who I want to be
I never knew so many could pray for another soul
When they should pray for their own in it there's a hole
Here is a little prayer each time you feel the urge
To tell someone they're wrong, your own truth you purge
Lord help me to mind my own like you showed me before
It's none of my business, I should know that for sure
And I'll shut my mouth the way I know I should
Not just for them I know it's for my own good
I'll stop digging in closets looking for others bones
Take the time to dig deep and clean out my own

Rhyme And The Reason

Why would a person take the time
To only speak with words that rhyme
It's hard to completely understand
With all the words we have at hand
No one could ever begin to know why
Until they sit and give it a try
It sounds to most like it's grade school
Just try and do it and not sound like a fool
It adds a challenge to the simple word
A unique way for thoughts to be heard
I love every minute, for my mind it's a test
Shake the words in my brain, use only the best
It makes us see more than just a thought
A word search in your head, each carefully sought
Exercise for the brain, stretch your vocabulary
To keep our mind sharp so necessary
Every word has a meaning, a use and a place
Be careful how you use them, use class and use grace
I hope this explains what I'm trying to do
These rhymes are for me as well as for you
They keep our minds sharp and seeking the truth
Things taught to us since the days of our youth
I don't do it alone, it comes from above
When I sit here stuck he sends down his love
Sends the right word when I fail to see
I would never think credit belongs to me
So think of this every single time
You sit and read the words that rhyme
The power of language that's what they speak
Bring smile, light and strength to the weak
Words contain power sometimes that's abused
Choose your words wisely and bombs are defused
Kind, thoughtful words are always in season
When we see life in the rhyme and the reason

THE ATHEIST

This is a true story and another one of the reasons I wrote this book. Owning a waterfowl hunting club led to meeting people from all over the country. We all had one thing in common, and that was a love for hunting waterfowl. It amazed me how many different walks of life and backgrounds could come together with such a binding bond through those birds. I've always enjoyed meeting people and this gave me the opportunity to listen to many different theories on life and all the things that go along with it. One day while sitting in a goose pit on a slow day, a man looked me in the eye and told me he was afraid he might be an atheist. He went on to say that he was the type of person that had to see something to believe it. He knew through previous conversation just how much I believed in God. He also knew how strong my convictions were and that made me wonder where this conversation was headed. As I looked down the pit I could see how serious he was, and I got the feeling he needed some real answers. I do remember thinking he might just be curious to see what I would say. But that feeling didn't last when I saw the look on his face. Either way, I knew this was a subject that was very important, and I didn't want to take my response lightly. The last thing that crossed my mind was he may really need me and he might be depending on how I describe how I feel.

I asked him what he meant, and he went on to tell me that he wasn't a proclaimed atheist like some. He told me that since he couldn't see God and couldn't believe in him that made him think he might be one. I will admit at that point in my life I believed strongly but had never been put in a position to explain what it meant to me. Over the years I had several conversations with people about God, but it had never seemed to be so urgent. I asked him what he thought about me believing without physically seeing God. He said he had tried to do that but just wasn't able to make himself do it. I asked him how much he knew about God, and he said basically God created the earth and if we were good people we would go to heaven, wherever that is. Then he added that, since he hadn't met anyone who had seen God, he couldn't make himself believe in Him either. I knew by the way he was talking that he was hoping I could help him believe. He wanted to believe, he just had never been able to. I think it may work that way for a lot of people. The whole time we were talking I remember thinking to myself, *how am I going to reach him in this obvious time of need.*

Then he asked me, "Just what is it was that makes you so sure that God does exist?"

I surprised myself when without hesitation I said "Everything." I could tell that it surprised him too when we both paused for a second to take that statement in. I think to this day that God himself provided that answer because it came too quickly and I hadn't even put any thought into it. I told him, "There isn't any one experience that led me to believe in God, it was more a chain of events that in time showed me how it all had been connected to God." The pressure was growing. I could feel it. This was really getting serious. The only thing I could think of next was to start asking him questions, "Have you heard that God is love?"

"Yes," he replied.

"Do you believe love is good?"

"Yes," he replied once more.

I said, "Well then we can say that God is good also." I told him I believed there was a reason why God and good were spelled similarly. The same thing can been seen with Devil and evil; that is no accident either. I could see he was still almost desperate for answers.

He leaned forward and said, "That still doesn't prove anything."

I asked him what he thought of the sunrise that morning. He said it was beautiful. "What do you think it was that allowed the two of us with different beliefs to come out here and realize the beauty of that sunrise this morning?" He just looked at me. I continued, "Something in our hearts and minds allowed us to appreciate that. That same love for the beautiful things in life we feel for creation is the same as what allows us to sit here and respect each other's opinions." I could tell I had said nothing to this point to make any difference at all. At the same time I noticed he was paying very close attention. I went on, "I know the birds we watched and everything else we enjoyed in every direction are all part of a beautiful creation. It's a creation so beautiful and perfect that every living thing has a place in the world. Food sources, shelter and abilities for all living things in my mind is no accident. I see every living thing depending on every other living thing and connected to each other in a way that makes all things necessary." I noticed he was starting to look with more intent, and I was still searching deeply in my mind for the right answers. I said, "I know there is a love or compassion in my heart to make me notice and appreciate these things. I know they are in you to or you wouldn't be out here appreciating it with me." He told me he would have to give me that one. I asked him if he thought that ability had been passed on to us by our father and mother as well as passed through them by theirs. Knowing what has been passed down from generation to generation, I have no choice but to believe it had to start somewhere. You know how I am when it comes to answers. I've spent most of my life searching just like everyone else. I have always been able to accept the fact that we don't know everything. I am not so sure that some things aren't better left that way. The unknown is just as capable of adding to our lives as the known. None of us will ever know what tomorrow brings. I told him that I knew for a fact that men a lot closer to the beginning of time believed enough to take notes and keep record. The words in the Bible alone are enough to prove to me that minds thousands of years ago were very educated. People were very aware of the difference between right and wrong. We actually seem to have slid backwards in recent years. Maybe not so much in our knowledge of it but our willingness to practice it has sure changed at all levels of society.

I could tell we were still not making much progress in him seeing God but we were agreeing on many of the things being talked about. He told me he could understand what I was saying but he still didn't feel like he could say he believed or could see God. I told him how it had always amazed me how people could witness the same event and walk away with different opinions on what they had seen. I told him, "The reason I think it is repeatedly written how important it is to believe and have faith is because it affects how we perceive the world. My belief is the reason why I saw God when I looked at that flock of birds. I saw God's work in that sunrise this morning. His beauty, grace and love is shown in everything here. No one can argue with the fact that the Bible truly is a blue print to a kinder, more fulfilling life. The longer I live, the more examples I've seen of just how true those words are. I can honestly say I have never seen words to be proven more profound in so many different ways for so many different people.

Once again I asked him if he was getting anything out of or conversation. He said "I agree with what you are saying I just wish someone could show Him to me in a way to erase any doubt I have in my mind."

"Well where are we," I asked. "We agree the bible exists, right? We agree the messages in the bible are good, right? We know it was passed from generation to generation to us, right? We know it was passed to us out of respect and admiration for God and the words in that book right? We know that the love passed down was done so because of that belief and faith we talked about, right? I think we can agree that no man holds the key to all the answers to all the questions facing us and this universe, right? So why would I assume I should be any different? I know I sure don't have all the answers right. Knowing I don't know everything, why wouldn't I turn to any source of advice on how to live. It is a fact that no source of information on life has ever been turned to, used, believed, trusted, passed down through time or proved to be more true for more people than that book. Why would I assume I know more in a time farther from the source than people who were there during those days?

"You must admit that the ideas in that book had to come from somewhere right. Well, people gave all that credit to God. How are you, me or anyone else today that wasn't there going to say we know more about that time than they did? They knew things about those days. We are only guessing what took place back then? Every year that goes by, we are guessing about those days even more than before. I have always been one to consider the source when I choose to take in or not take in information. When it comes to the information in that book, I believe the people who were there know more about what happened than all those who try to make educated guesses. I know how seriously the people who passed these words down took them. That leads me to believe there is more to it than just what I think I might know. I have never been so pretentious as to think I do, should or ever will know everything.

"Being someone who is always searching for the truth I study everything. I had to find the things I know to be true. It is so difficult to put it in terms others can understand. The more of these facts that are known to be true about love and its origin, the better foundation we have to start building our faith on. That foundation was made strong by my family. Experiences in my life have all been evaluated and compared to the words and thoughts in the bible. Over the years, my faith and belief system has been altered and enhanced by the occurrences that have happened within my life. Every time I compare my life with His word, I have been able to see the connection. Trust me when I say I have spent as much time as anyone trying to prove or disprove those words. Maybe it was that solid foundation given to me by my family. It could have been the fact that they believed the way they did. Whatever it was, it gave me the start I needed and I think it gave me a better understanding of how to look. Whatever it is, my life experiences have never proven those words not to be true. Many times they have done just the opposite and proven to me more than ever how prophetic those words are. I become more amazed each year at the fact that words spoken and written so many years ago can be proven to be true as well as provide a better way to live.

"Once I determined the facts that I knew to be true, I had no choice but to believe some of the things others still question. I know love exists. I know the bible exists. I know people who model their life after it are kinder more enjoyable people to be around. The thoughts are good. The people are good. Love is good. All those things are good, and they all come from a God's book. Therefore God is good. And I've come to believe over the years that God truly is love. That is when I decided if love is real and the thoughts of it are real, then I can see God just as real. Once I came to realize this, I decided all acts of love came through God. It's not even a question for me anymore. I have had many experiences in my life and connecting them all together has led me to believe what I do today. I feel blessed simply for the fact that, while we live in a time of great knowledge and so many seem to struggle with the truth, I have been led to a place where I am comfortable with what I know about God and love.

"That is the way I came to know I could see him everywhere. Knowing so many acts of kindness and love over the years and inspired by his word, I am able to see Him and His words in every act of kindness. That brought me to a point in my life to be able to see him for myself in you and others. For me, every act of kindness I have ever witnessed is directly from Him. I really do see Him in your face with every act of kindness you give. That is how I started seeing Him everywhere. That is also how I started seeing His face in the faces of many."

This was starting to become a lot to take in. As I waited to see his response, I could see his wheels turning. He said, "You mean after me telling you I might be an atheist you're telling me you can still see God in my face."

"Yes sir, I sure do." There was a short moment where neither of us spoke. We just kind of looked at each other in silence. This time I could see a different look on his face. I could actually see him giving my words considerable thought. Just the fact he was thinking about what I had said made me feel a little better. I could tell by his face he was giving it careful consideration. The thing I noticed most was his look of concern had turned into a look of thought. I knew he couldn't argue with most of what I had said. I had a feeling it would be better not to add anymore at this time. I started asking him questions about the way he felt about what I had just said.

He told me that he still didn't feel he could see God, but he could understand what I was saying and how I felt as if I could. I told him another way I knew was the fact I had been given this information at a very early age. I had been taught quite well where and how to look by my family. And I knew that was a blessing in itself. Armed with the right information at such an early age had given me more time to test those words and to know them to be true. Every act of kindness I see, I see as coming through generations of believers. I know the only way people could have held on so tight for so long was the way those words must have influenced their life. It's strange to me, believing what I do, that people don't seem to see Him as clearly as I do. I couldn't deny Him if I tried. I don't understand why anyone would want to. Why would anyone waste time trying to find fault in something that has worked so well for so many for so long. Maybe one of the reasons I see Him so much is because I expect to. It's no longer an option for me.

I found my way to believing at an early age because I was given very good advice from adults who had that same advantage from the adults in their life. I will always feel that people that find truth in him at an early age, did so not because of their own intelligence but because of the things they were taught to look for. Most people are looking for a man. What we are talking about is love. Love takes on many forms, just as God does. Unlike a lot of people, I am not looking for a man. I am looking for the thought, emotion, action and results from the words in that book. The book speaks of love, and I have always felt that to be the message. Love is the concept and the pages are filled with the knowledge we need to achieve it. It doesn't matter who or what you choose to call the origin of where these thoughts came from. God, the father, Jesus or the great creator, no one can argue the fact they will lead you to a better life. As for me personally, I don't think the reason to live by those words should be to get ourselves into heaven. At least that is not why I do it. I do it because I have found it to be the most rewarding thing I have ever done. I find love, peace and joy inside myself when I share with, care for and love others.

After several minutes of a very serious conversation, I smiled and said, "I'm not saying I am right and you are wrong. I'm just telling you how I feel and believe." He smiled back and told me for the first time he thought someone had at least given him something to think about. I laughed and said one thing I thought for sure was we weren't the first to think about these things, and we sure wouldn't be the last. One thing I noticed almost immediately was that look of concern and doubt had been replaced with a more satisfied look of thought. I remember thinking at that time, even if I hadn't shown him God as he had hoped I could, I had given him something to think about just as my family had given to me.

I asked him if anything I had said helped. I became very encouraged when he said, "I still won't say I can see or believe in God." But he said in the same breath, "I do understand how you say you came to see him and you have given me something to think about." Just the thought of him being willing to think about it gave me hope he might learn to see for himself.

Just as our conversation had started, it ended. Back to the task at hand we finished out our hunt enjoying the day and all that came with it. That evening as we loaded everything up for him to return home his hunting partner came up and said, "I really enjoyed the conversation you two had." He told me, "I have believed just as you do most of my life also. We have had several conversations on that topic over the years. I don't think I have ever seen him give it that much consideration. I don't know if you convinced him but you surely convinced me." He got in the truck and prepared for the long drive home.

My misbelieving friend hadn't heard our conversation and I didn't bring it up. Almost six hours after our talk he brought it up again. He said he had been thinking about what I had said and maybe he had been seeing God but just never had looked at it in the right way. He said he would keep the things I had said in mind and see if he could see what I was claiming to see. He was actually looking forward to looking at it from a different angle. The last thing he said to me before he left was thank you. He said no one had ever explained it to him that way as far as what he should be looking for to see God. I called him by name and told him I hoped I had helped in some way and I was sorry if I hadn't.

As always, another year passed and another waterfowl season had come. It was his friend that booked the hunt every year. When he called he told me he didn't know if his buddy was going to be able to make it.

He hadn't said why, he only said he didn't know. When the day came only one of them pulled into the parking lot. The first thing I asked him was where is your buddy? His smile quickly disappeared and I could tell it wasn't good. As it happens all too often these days, he proceeded to tell me his friend had cancer. I instantly thought of our conversation the previous year. If he didn't know he had cancer then he must have had a feeling. That would explain the sudden interest in God and why I had become so sure in my own convictions. We said a prayer for him and proceeded into the field for our hunt.

Throughout the day we would discuss him and his situation. I learned that in the past couple of months he had several talks with his friend about the conversation we had the year before. He told me I had really made a difference in him and he even spoke of feeling as if he had been seeing and hearing from God. He had spoken of seeing Him in some of his friends. He said that a couple of the nurses taking care of him had shown him God's love and he could almost see God in their faces, just as I had explained. I remember how good it felt to think maybe I had made a difference for him. I also thought at one point that maybe I needed to sit down for my own good and try to simplify this very controversial matter. I wondered how someone could have lived for over sixty years without anyone being able to give him an answer he could feel satisfied with. I also remember thinking, maybe he just never took the time to look very hard in the first place.

We finished out the day and I returned home to call and check in on my doubting friend. He sounded pretty good over the phone but the words he spoke to me were what really eased my mind. After our initial hello and a quick medical update he immediately turned the conversation. He told me, "Thank you so much for taking time to explain your thoughts and feelings on God. I spent most of my life never thinking about it. When this first came upon me I started wondering. No one I asked could explain anything to me that gave me comfort. Your thoughts and words that day in the pit really changed me. Without really trying I just started seeing things differently. It didn't take long at all before I actually felt like I was seeing evidence of him. I understand how you say you can see him in others. I know I have seen him in a couple of the people taking care of me. "

He was so eager to tell me examples of what he now believed to be Gods love. His words left me almost speechless. Even though I had seen the urgency in his eyes that day in the field, I never imagined I could make such a difference in someone's life with simple words. I told him how good it made me feel to think I might of helped him in some way. I wished him the very best with his fight and hung up the phone.

He is still fighting his battle, according to the last I heard. I find myself thinking of him and praying for him often. I always get a good feeling when I think of how grateful his words had been. Even though I realized the importance of our conversation when it took place that day in the pit, I never dreamed those few minutes could have that much impact on someone's life. The last time I spoke with him he thanked me. He told me that he could actually tell people he could see and talk to God as well as believe it for himself. He was confident he is going to beat this and confident that, no matter what happens, God will be with him. Without talking to him, I always wonder if he is still here. I have to keep checking in with him or his friends for my own piece of mind. As of a few weeks ago his progress has been for the better.

Those few minutes in the field that winter day have become a big part of my life. It has always amazed me how so little time or effort can have so much impact on our lives. His story became our story that day, and I know it is one that will stick with me forever. I am so thankful that God sent me the words to help reach him in his time of need. The satisfaction that comes to me through his story leaves me wanting more. The very reason for this book is the hope of anyone like him out there finding a way to believe in God. It truly was God's grace at work guiding our conversation. For that particular situation, through Him the right questions were asked and the right answers offered. It really was a miracle that took place that morning. It changed all three of us for the better. I know it was God, because I am no miracle worker; He is. The change I witnessed in this man in such a short period of time told me that this radical change is possible for others too.

There is power in the Word. I don't believe any man can ever truly know just how much power there is. I know I can say I have seen some of this power. I can also say I will spend the rest of my days trying to unleash that power for others. My life has been blessed, and I have no doubt that it is do to the fact I have been seeing him for a long time. My only intention for telling this story is to share that fact with you. Many of you already know of what I am speaking. It's the ones like him I hope to reach. There are many more people like him that are discouraged by the things they have seen or the people doing the explaining. It is very complex and we often have a tendency to make things seem more difficult instead of less. I've said it before and I'll say it again, it's not just a matter of looking but the way we look that is just as important. I have also noticed that the way I explained my personal opinions to him might not be the best way to explain it to someone else. Pushing fifty years old, I have seen enough examples of God's love in my life that there is no doubt in my mind anymore. I really do see Him in everyone at times. I grow more grateful every day for the people in my life that taught me how to look many years ago. I've learned my experiences are not like anyone else's. The way I see those experiences is very different than some. I'm not claiming to know everything, but I do claim this way of looking has worked very well for me. I have been very blessed my whole life, and no one will ever convince me God has not been working in my life. Instead, I will tell what I know to be true for me to others in the hope someone else will find a more joyful life. It is possible for us all to have that life, but we will never know or see him without truly knowing how to look. The one thing I want to leave you with is this thought. The next time you do not feel his presence or feel the need to say he does not exist, stop and take a good look around. I'll bet he is at work right before your eyes. If you know what God stands for, you will start seeing him everywhere.

Short Quotes

These days it's easier to take the high road. The low road is way too congested.

Don't stir the pot, unless you are prepared to get the ingredients in your face.

Two heads are only better than one when they both have some intelligence.

Have you noticed how much brighter some life's shine than others?

So-called convenient memory lapses are really truths untold. We all know what God thinks about that.

I like to see myself as God's greatest gift maybe just damaged a little during shipping.

Always follow God. Don't follow me or anyone else for that matter.

I've noticed brains aren't standard equipment. Apparently they are optional.

You are judgmental and hypocritical if you see attention from a desirable person as charming and the same attention from an undesirable person as harassment.

God said love thy neighbor. Aren't you glad certain people don't live next to you?

If God didn't have a sense of humor, I don't know if you would be here.

I've done everything I've ever wanted to with my life. I probably failed at most of it.

Spend your time cleaning your own closet, and stay out of everyone else's.

If I had a dollar for every time I was right I would have to have invested in all the times I was wrong to have a shot at becoming a millionaire.

I survived my kids, but I'm afraid society is going to have to toughen up.

I used all my youth and energy learning how to spend my time. Now I know, but I don't have the energy.

This may not be a deep pond. It may be more like a shallow puddle.

Mother-in-law! Not by choice, that's why they made it a law.

Sorry I'm taken. I started ruining someone else's life years ago.

For every eagle that soars from the nest, a slower one falls over the edge.

How happy do happy people have to be before they are considered to be special?

Look close, listen hard and speak less!

When blaming everyone else fails, just try looking in the mirror.

Count your blessings not your bitchings!

If you don't know how much you love your wife, just ask her. I'm sure she will be more than glad to tell you (I'll bet it's not as much as you thought it was).

What do women want? I'll have to get back to you on that one. I'm still waiting for them to figure it out.

Did you say no one listens to you? I wasn't paying attention.

If you are so certain that you know everything, then how do you explain missing time to shut up?

I'm really not that stupid. I'm a genius in disguise.

If you can't then get out of the way and get me an I can.

We decided to cut the bad limbs out of our family tree. Now it's the family telephone pole.

The best of your abilities should go into your first attempt.

Our marriage is just as beautiful as it ever was. We just meet a little farther south these days.

Don't tell me your problems. Fix them!

Isn't it ironic the person who usually makes the least sense is the one threatening to knock it into you?

God's world is still beautiful! You just have to go a lot farther to find a place man hasn't messed it up yet.

My wife says these prove that I'm nothing without her. Oh well, she forgets I had no problem being nothing before we met.

The greatest thing about America is we can give glory to God anytime we choose to.

People that want to know your problems are afraid to deal with their own.

A good relationship is when two people can live together without smothering the life out of one another.

Try something different! Tell people to do what they want to do instead of what you want them to do.

You don't demand respect. You have to earn it.

You can't demand trust. It must be earned.

Smile, even if you don't want to!

If you feel the need to tell others what to do, I bet the best thing for you is to shut up and do it yourself.

Sometimes when people are struggling, it's easier for them to take pride in themselves after someone else does for no apparent reason.

Politicians don't lie. They just tell it like they want it to be.

Maybe they aren't inadequate. Maybe you are one of those people who are never pleased.

Sometimes it's hard to see how wrong we are when we see ourselves so right.

To tell the truth you have to remember nothing. To tell a lie you better be able to remember everything.

Stop being so nervous! You are human. We all already know you're not perfect.

No matter how far you roam, every trip ends with "there is no place like home."

Odds are, you are only wrong two to three times more often than you think you are.

Don't take yourself too seriously. I promise you no one else is.

If you think having class is being just like you, then I would have to say I don't have it and I don't want it.

The Farmers Prayer

He sits on the farm, surrounded by God's favor
A promise made to him for the fruits of his labor
The size of the farm matters the least
Each inch of soil turned in hope of a feast
It's a joint effort between God and man
Down here on earth the farmer does what he can
The creak in his bones the sweat of his brow
Work through day and night, his work is done now
Back from the field, one thing left to do
Drop down to his knees and look up to you
Each farmer's words may vary and waiver
But they all come to you in the name of the Savior
Eagerly he watches out over his field
As God does the same while preparing the yield
Your sun and your wind, your soil and your rain
Turned things from brown back to green again
As he stands here today their efforts evident and binding
The truth in the word is what he is finding
The farmer gives thanks, praise and glory to God
I feel sorry for the lost, who see that as odd
It truly is a blessing each and every meal
God and man work together, that's what seals the deal
If you fail to see this before you sit to eat
Then you missed a great blessing laid down at your feet
Thank God and the farmer then let it be said
God's promise and the farmer's faith give us our daily bread

OUR DIFFERENCES

Someone is pushing us in the wrong direction,
Hoping we fail to make the connection.
Everyone seeking the same destination,
People today and way back to creation.
The thing that makes the world a better place:
Different thoughts and ideas, different heritage and race.
Learn from each other with peace face to face,
Accepting each other, it's simply God's grace.
True forward progress all comes from that.
His plan speaks true wisdom, not idle chat.
A new way of seeing the world round, not flat.
Keep tolerance alive or watch it beat to the mat.
Acceptance under attack everyday now.
I don't understand why or exactly how.
Now every night when my head I bow.
I pledge to accept, not throw in the towel.
Imagine every life on an island alone,
Written word of another all to be known.
Size, shape, sex and skin color not shown.
Only mind mattered the rest could be stone.
Tolerance still practiced by many no doubt.
No differences of others do they speak or point out.
Those who judge others the differences they shout.
Fail to know God and what he's all about.
I've heard together we stand, divided we fall.
Though the thought may be the message not small.
Do you really believe that you'll get the call?
Failing his test, the most important of all.
He created before birth what he wished to see.
Ways we can think and ways we can be.
We all have the right to live our life free.

No one with the right to take that from me.
If a better life is something you thirst.
Stop passing judgment, things you do it's the worst.
So many blessings your heart may burst.
When you put yourself last, he'll bless you first.

How Bright is Your Light

Every life on God's green earth
Carry his light from the day of birth
How bright we shine is no guarantee
Too bright to look or too dim to see
Light is determined by how much we love
Brighter when we look for guidance from above
Light will shine brighter when used for others
Our children and friends, sisters and brothers
When left all alone the light starts to fade
Sharing light with others the energy is made
All lights burn brighter when there's harmony
The music that's made like a great symphony
Many can dance when we share the light
Every last soul can reach a new height
Everyone knows of a light growing dim
Are you willing to share your light with them
An awesome feeling comes over your soul
Use your light for another you start to glow
A great feeling you get not at all odd
Passed back to you is the light from God
We all shine bright with his understanding
But get lost in the dark when we are demanding
The one thing I've noticed the longer I live
You have more, not less the more that you give
Our light alone usually shines in one direction
There is more than one path to a life of perfection
Start with the path God shines his light down
I'll bet at the end he left you a crown
Light from above holds so much power
You feel it changing yours hour by hour
Yours burning brighter with His added to it
Light a path for another that's how you do it

Brighter and brighter the darkness becomes
Shining the way to new found freedoms
God's love is the light with more than enough
To turn dark into light and weak into tough
With his light in ours we help spread the word
More lights turned on when his message is heard
If you don't speak of God and all He can do
No lights turned on because of you too
Do the lights in your life shine brighter today
Do you have any power in the things that you say
God's light will shine on your darkest night
Show you the way, it's a wonderful sight

Look With Intention

I'm starting to tire of the comments of doubt
So many out there still trying to figure it out
I don't understand how it can be
Look everyday and still they can't see
The failure to see comes from within
A new way of looking they need to begin
Looking in anger you will only see hate
Change that outlook before it seals your fate
Eyes that are sad notice only the pain
I know that in this there is nothing to gain
Looking with hurt you'll see ways to get back
Vengeance is God's, forgive don't attack
Looking unsure never leads us to right
Unable to choose between dark and light
Scared eyes only show you a place to hide
Unable to relax and enjoy the ride
Doubtful eyes seem to never find you
Trusting you are there they just can't do
Evil eyes are always the worst kind
Work of the Devil they have in mind
None of these ways to see all of life
All ways that only add to the strife
Look with compassion before you will see it
With it in your eyes that's what you'll get
See with understanding you'll know where you are needed
It leads to other hearts, their garden needs weeded
Eyes looking with hope find a way to get through
Share it with others for that helps them too
Seeing with faith shows you there is hope
That is what's needed when it's tough to cope
If you have been blessed eyes that see with love
I know you've been touched by God up above

When you search for Him, with which eyes do you look?
What matters most, at least the message I took
Look the wrong way, you might as well be blind
You'll look all your life but you never will find
See him everywhere when you look through right eyes
Look the same way, He looks down from the skies
Knowing eyes expect to see Him, that I must mention
See him when you want when you look with intention

His Song for the Children

God told me today
Listen what I say
On your knees and pray
Then carry on your way

What He said to do
Take time to help you
Not feel quite so blue
I should wear your shoe

That way I can find
Peace in my own mind
Acts we do in kind
Helps us all unwind

He said shed a tear
Told me not to fear
Help another hear
Then we all can cheer

I heard what he said
Use what's in your head
Get out of that bed
Live until your dead

Acts you should insert
Give someone your shirt
No one's feelings hurt
Rise up from the dirt

Tell all that you see
What you hear from me
The only way to be
It will set you free

Now before I go
One more thing to show
It's what makes us glow
Everyone should know

Gentle as the dove
What I'm speaking of
My gift from above
Just go out and love

God's Guidance (Ma's Prayer)

Just like God stepped in and guided us when we didn't know
where to be or what to do. I have no doubt he will be there
to guide your mom home. It's hard sometimes to believe, no matter how
strongly we have done so our whole life. Those are
The times when he makes himself seen and sends us his angels
to guide us. If we keep our eyes and hearts open without hiding or looking
away, we can see that almost everywhere we look. God
and his angels are at work right now with you and for you to bring
peace and comfort back into your heart. He was here to guide our
steps yesterday as he will be there to guide your mom home
tomorrow. My thoughts, my prayers and my love are with you
and Ma. I love you.

MUSIC

Let me tell you how I came to find
Only two types of music up in my mind
I can't believe most the people I meet
Pick only one kind with all at their feet
The two I speak of are good and bad
I find it in all types since I was a lad
How much melody is one going to miss
To say of music I only listen to this
Since the first man took a stick and a stump
Slapped them together in a rhythmic thump
Music stirred the soul of that early man
So broaden your horizon as wide as you can
Songs send a message deep into your soul
The urge to stomp is so hard to control
I still stir to the beat of the tom toms
Music inspires and teaches, riles or calms
Every instrument with a time and place
Music that's good puts a smile on your face
Message in the lyrics determines which type
With no message of God it's only hype
Like the sweet sound of Amazing Grace
It sooths the heart when it's heaven you chase
Sounds that inspire and lead to decision
Different point of view, another man's vision
In all categories I've found many good songs
That's why we listen for those our heart longs
Rock, country, folk, Christian and R&B
Some amazing talent in all I can see
Picture the violin, the saw and the jug
Music of the past will give your heart a tug
Since the beginning man had something to say
In all types of music, I hear that today

Some judge all music just like they do people
Accept only the song sung under their steeple
How much space must be left in the heart
When hearing from all we fail to start
Don't be surprised when you ride with me
Today it's Christian rock, tomorrow it's R&B
Constantly searching for songs with good message
They lead us all to our right of passage
Open your mind when it comes to the song
More accepting of others, I bet won't take you long
It adds to the insight and from where it comes
More in our life when we total the sums
Most proudly admit they only favor one
Sadly, I see about most they know none
It doesn't surprise me some do it with music
They do it with people, now that's really sick
I think the point or at least what I'm hopin'
Our minds and our hearts should be more open
If you like only country then you should know
A lot of it today came from rock and roll
The creative today combine and evolve
Differences and categories start to dissolve
To me that is what marks a real progress
Guiding us all from the divided mess
Embracing the music might help embracing others
Instead of those over there, we only see brothers

Music shows others how we feel inside
Shows in each life how they choose to ride
I want a good life so the songs that I pick
Send a good message one that will stick
Words that agree with the one up above
Songs that shout out a message of love
They can be easy or rock the night away
Whatever goes with the mood that's what I play

IT

TAKE IT, GIVE IT, SEEK IT,
FIND IT, KEEP IT, SHARE IT,
HOLD IT, SQUEEZE IT, KNOW IT,
SHOW IT, WIN IT, LOOSE IT,
BREAK IT, FIX IT,
CHOOSE IT, USE IT, WRITE IT,
SPEAK IT, FEEL IT, BE IT,
SEE IT, HEAR IT, TOUCH IT, TASTE IT,
START IT, BEND IT, LEARN IT,
TEACH IT, PREACH IT, REACH IT,
FAKE IT, BLIND IT, HURT IT,
HEAL IT, MEAN IT, CLEAN IT,
TEST IT, PASS IT, GUARD IT,
TRUST IT, LEAVE IT, MISS IT,
SHAPE IT, MOLD IT, MIX IT,
BLEND IT, TRY IT, DO IT, CUT IT,
NURSE IT, CURSE IT, BLESS IT,
HIDE IT, LIGHT IT, PUSH IT,
PULL IT, MAKE IT, LIKE IT,
LIVE IT, LOVE IT,
IT COMES FROM ABOVE
ALL ALONG IT IS LOVE

IT COMES FROM ABOVE
ALL ALONG IT IS LOVE

Short Quotes

Stop and smell the roses before you mow them over like everything else

Don't count your chickens until they are on the table

Enjoy life while it is still happening

It's better to dance poorly than to choose to sit and watch

My poor wife, just knowing myself makes my heart go out to her

These days you have to speak softly and carry a gun

In America, even you can become president

If you ask me, your demands sound a lot like your problems

Every man, woman and child are beautiful but some just become less attractive when they speak

If they raised the IQ number for mental competency by two points, would you be one of the new ones drawing disability

There is no greater way to spend your time than loving and caring for other people

If you want to see Jesus right here on Earth, just look into the eyes of a small child

Believe in God, love your family, love your friends and keep your judgment of others to yourself

I give everyone the benefit of doubt. For how long is determined on an individual basis

Enjoy today. If tomorrow comes, odds are someone will screw it all up somehow

Bring back the paddle and respect will come back on it's own

Being a genuine good role model for kids is the most important thing you will ever do

Believe it or not, you will miss your kids when they are grown and gone, but only for short periods of time

My wife has so many rules I suggested she work for the government

Hot air flows freely. People full of it never shut up

Everyday is a good day, some are just better than others

Don't complain. No one listens when you do. They just pretend to while they wish you would shut up

Enjoy the sunrise; stop complaining about it hurting your eyes on the way to work

There is so much power in the tongue. It can cut to the bone or heal the deepest wounds

Love keeps us together even when all the hate around us is trying to break us apart

I don't hate anyone, but I will say I have to love some people in smaller amounts

I think God's love is beyond most human perception

Love is everywhere, but unconditional love is hard to find

Most people can't walk in someone else's shoes. They try, but even then they can only see how that affects themselves

In some countries you can still be shot for writing or even thinking stuff like this

Only with 100% honesty will it ever truly be God's love

Look out for yourself. No one else has as much to lose in you as you do

Love being alive while you still are, it's the only way to live when you consider the options

People matter most

Treat people like you wish to be treated. When someone mistreats you, and they will, you need to keep doing it anyway

You can be first if you want to, but first you must ask yourself if you are willing to put more effort into it than second

Have you noticed how most people when blamed just start looking for someone else and pass it on

If "because I said so" is a reason, then shouldn't "because I want to" be one too

Sorry, I can't tell you what you want to hear, I can only tell you what God told me and what I think about it

How ironic! You don't think I'm funny and I don't think you have a sense of humor

I love you even when you hate me

I'm not simple minded or ignoring the situation. The answers just aren't that difficult. Stop making them that way

Don't blame God when you find yourself at the end of a road He encouraged you not to take.

Puppies are great! But, if you hide behind them and love them more than people, your life really has gone to the dogs

Made your own mind; made your own choice. Made your own way; now you've made your own pile. Stop flinging it at everyone else.

The problem with holidays is the fact you managed to avoid some of those people all year long.

You think it's difficult being you. You should try being one of us and have to listen to you

Real intelligence is often attempted, rarely achieved and mostly faked.

I missed the scripture where God put me here so you could tell me what to do.

If you don't like me and feel the need to express it, odds are the feeling is mutual. So, save your breath.

We are different! Get over it! I don't want you to be me, so stop trying to turn me into you.

If you don't want to flow with the current, then, tell us all, what are you doing on the river.

Women and children are God's most beautiful creations when they smile. They are his favorite when they smile. That's why he stresses many times in his words to watch over them and do things to make them smile. When you do this you make Him smile.

Money's not the root of all evil. It can actually be used to do great things. It's the people that will do anything for money that are the root of all evil.

Nothing I say or do should make you feel bad. Only your conscience can do that.

Jealousy is the emotion responsible for most personal attacks.

Don't brag about how good things are going for you. That's not what most people want to hear anyway.

Pretend to be someone your not and you will forget who you really are.

Our differences should be celebrated not condemned.

If someone has to change to be what you want, then maybe they are not what you really want and you should leave them alone.

If you can't laugh at yourself, then you probably shouldn't be laughing so hard at everybody else.

If you wish to be entertained by good thoughts, read this book. If you wish to grow in God, read the bible.

You sit there and tell me you don't believe in him, and then turn around and ask me my advice on why nothing is working out for you. Think about it. I'll bet even you can figure this one out on your own.

When you look in the mirror and pick out the things you think make you weak, I see those things as making you unique.

I've never turned my back on a child. I have turned my back on a few adults acting like one though.

God didn't give us cars, boats, jet ski's and roller coasters to enjoy. He gave us life and each other to enjoy.

I still pledge, I still pray and I still spank when need be.

If life doesn't seem to be going your way, maybe it's you that needs to change your destination.

Life is awesome, amazing, mystical, magical and fleeting! Live it!

Other people's choices aren't yours to make!

Intolerance is the only thing we should not tolerate!

You can judge me and the words in this book. You can even claim God is taking your side as you come against me. With my knowledge of Him, I wont judge you back or come against you!

These are my thoughts, my words, my opinions and my book. You're more than welcome to your own.

I have no intention of telling you what to do. I'm telling you what I do!

Out of the Fire

On a hot July evening in the year 2001 our family experienced a home fire. Thankfully, no one was home. My wife, my son, my daughter and I are all alive and well today. It was a night that was burned into our minds forever. In many ways, it changed all of us for the better. Who and where we are now would not be as good as it is now, if not for that fire. What we all witnessed in the weeks following that fire was nothing short of amazing. My family witnessed more acts of God's love, caring and giving in those weeks than one can even begin to imagine.

As I mentioned, it was hot. Little league season had just come to an end. My son was staying with a friend. My wife, my daughter and I had been out playing catch in the backyard. All three of us were dressed in T-shirts and shorts. The party for our ball team was to be the next day. We had picked up the girls' trophies and were discussing what needed done before the party. It was a pool party and our daughter wanted to go pick out a new swimming suit. My wife and I decided to take her to the mall and let her pick one out. It was getting late so we didn't change, we just jumped in the truck. My wife ran inside to make sure everything was turned off and locked up.

The ride to the mall was all-good. Talk of the season, the party and more free time now that baseball was over carried us from store to store. My daughter had to find just the right one and that late in the season the selections were dwindling. We weren't in a hurry anyway. It was just more family time spent together and we all enjoyed that. When she found the one she wanted, we all exited the mall with smiles on our faces. We strolled across the lot and jumped in the truck, eager to return home. I don't think at that time anyone of us had a care in the world. We started up the truck and headed for the house.

I can remember interrupting the conversation about halfway home when I noticed a huge plume of black smoke coming from town. I can still remember to this day my exact words. "There is one hell of a fire in Herrin, "I said. You could tell it was really big. Conversation the rest of the way home remained about all the smoke and hope that everyone was out safe.

When we got further into town, we could see it was on our side. None of us had a clue what we were about to pull up to. Remember, it's getting late and we are all ready to go home. It's time to call it a day.

I also can remember getting an uneasy feeling sitting at the stoplights waiting to cross Park Avenue. I remember looking at my wife and saying, "That's our neighborhood". We had three more blocks to be home, at least that's what we thought. When the light turned green, I looked at my wife and saw a look of panic begin to come over her face. We started dreading every turn of the tires towards home. When we turned onto our street the rug was jerked out from beneath us.

I had barely straightened the wheel when I saw a fireman run around her car dragging a hose, and I said, "It's our house; it's our house that's on fire." I will never forget the sunken feeling that set in at that very moment. I will also never forget the moment that immediately followed.

From the back seat our daughter began screaming in horror, "Yellow! Yellow! I have to get Yellow!" Yellow was her hamster and that was the very first thought that entered her head. She was hysterical. It makes my eyes tear up still to this day when I think of that moment. I can't imagine what her little heart must have been feeling. I can still hear that shrill voice as if it were happening right now. Listening to her and seeing what was happening right before our eyes was too much for my wife to take. She immediately started breaking down. This was definitely a lot to take in. I drove the three blocks to our street unable to speak. Every inch of the way the cries and the screams got more desperate and numbing. Our street was blocked off so I had to pull in the alley behind our neighbor's house across the street.

As we exited the truck, my daughter was kicking and screaming trying to get into the house to save her hamster. My wife was going into shock as we walked between the houses to get to ours. At first I didn't notice all the people. Walking up my eyes could only see the flames, and my ears could only hear the cries of my wife and daughter. Family and friends quickly surrounded both of them, so I kept approaching our burning home. I know people were approaching me and speaking. I can't tell you if I spoke back. In a state of shock, I couldn't get my mind to stop spinning and focus. I still don't know how we got those last three blocks to our house. There is probably about fifteen minutes that are completely lost in my mind.

The first group of people I noticed was a small group of firemen sitting in the street. They looked like they had just gone fifteen rounds in a title fight. The heat of the day and the intensity of the fire had almost done them in. Most of them were good friends of ours. One I had coached ball with for three or four years. As I approached I noticed he had tears in his eyes along with the smoke and the sweat. "Thank God they are with you! We didn't know! Your truck was gone so we figured you were out, but with her car here we were afraid she might be home with the kids. We haven't been able to get in, its too far gone and way too strong." You could see the relief in his face as well as the love in his heart that was going out to us. Looking back, I can now see how those guys were in a state of shock as well. Up to that point, it had become too much to take in. I know for a period of time my mind was lost. I think that short conversation kind of snapped me back to reality.

For the first time I noticed all the people. I noticed a look of shock on all the faces. My attention immediately turned back to my wife and kids. It ruined me to look upon them so broken and hurt. For my daughter there was no thought of possessions, only the loss of her hamster's life. Beyond our loss, our situation and our pain, my wife had added guilt. She convinced herself she had left tea on the stove or a candle burning. I know the mind can do things we don't yet understand. How or why she was so quick to take the blame I don't know. Maybe someone had asked her if she had done one of those things. All I know is, she was convinced it was her fault and there was nothing I could say to comfort her. Back with my wife and daughter, I was just beginning to comprehend how broken we all were.

Some situations leave nothing that can be said or done. This was one of those times. All we can do is watch and learn. So that's what we did. Along with family, friends and neighbors we watched. Everyone was just standing, watching and thinking. It's strange, but there was a common ground we were all standing on at that point and time. It was our home that was lost, but the concern, the caring, and the love was evident to everyone there. Something like that hits close to home for everybody. You start thinking how it could have been you, and start getting a better understanding of what is taking place. All the emotions and prayers shared by so many in the same location is what I believe responsible for what happened next. God's angels began to make their presence known. They showed up one by one at first. In no time at all, they began to come to us in flocks. As our home still burned before us, these angels began pouring God's blessings into our hearts and minds. We realized he had blessed us before it even started by making sure we were all gone and in a safe place. Later we learned the fire had started at the entrances to our kids' bedrooms. I try not to think what might have happened had we all been home in bed asleep.

While we all stood and watched the fire, angels started approaching my wife and handing her money. It was hard for me to accept the fact people felt pity for us. It was hard for me to be the one being helped. We had spent our whole life helping others. My pride told me we would be just fine, even though it was fairly easy to see we were going to need all the help we could get. It's a tough pill to swallow when you have taken pride your whole life for being able to take care of it ourselves. I truly believed at that time we would overcome this just like we had everything else in the past twenty years. The angels disagreed and told us we were going to need all the help we could get. It seemed it was as important to them to help us as it was to me to do it myself. People we had never met walked down the street just to offer their support. I'm still amazed by the fact that, within minutes of our darkest moments, we were seeing acts of God's kindness and love coming into our life. Even more amazing is the fact that we were realizing this with everything that could be so distracting to that fact. Just as amazing as that is the fact everyone there that night could see and feel it. All I know for sure is what took place from that point on was nothing less than mystical and magical. God's love has never poured into our lives in so many ways from so many people at one time. Not just that night, but for weeks God's angels lined up to deliver his blessings.

It was the early morning hours before the flames were extinguished and the show was over. A couple of firemen took us in so we could retrieve my guns and her jewelry. Dad suggested plywood for the doors and windows. Not to protect our stuff. There was none. Mainly, he wanted to keep kids from getting in there and hurting themselves. The firemen asked us not to incase there was a flare up and they had to come back. They told us to get some rest. They said between them and the police they would be keeping an eye on it.

Before the fire was out we had at least a half a dozen places to stay offered to us: empty rental properties, camping trailers, spare bedrooms and both our parent's homes. It made me proud to think of all the good friends the four of us have made in the twenty years we had been a family. I told my wife one time, "It was a good thing we spent those years building bridges instead of burning them." That night we moved in with Mom and Dad. At the same time though we were realizing we needed a place to stay.

We also realized we didn't have anything to pack and take anywhere. For the first time, I took a look at all of us and clearly saw that what we were wearing is everything we own. I look down at my old T-shirt, cut off jeans, sandals and my one pair of Fruit of the Looms. I can tell you for a fact whether God is in your life or not, that is not a good feeling.

Back at Mom and Dad's we sat down for the first time since we had jumped out of the truck nearly seven hours earlier. That's when a different kind of shock began to set in. Unlike the kind that is filled with high adrenaline and many mixed emotions, this was very different. This was more of a numb thoughtless feeling that left us just sitting and gazing with a blank stare. It was like a tornado taking over our minds with thoughts twirling around too fast for us to take the time to make any sense out of. It reminded me of a silent movie playing back images in my head with no dialog and no apparent plot. It makes you think about just how remarkable the human brain is and how little we truly understand about its abilities. We are unable to know what our own mind is capable of until it is pushed farther than it has been pushed before. Often we end up surprised at our own abilities when situations test us.

We lived at Mom and Dad's for fifty-seven days waiting for the home we are in now to be ready. It was difficult on all of us. I was grateful for how smoothly everything went during those days. We all managed very well to get along and it made our transition period go so much smoother. Mom and Dad, once again I say thank you so much for being there for us. We could have never felt so comfortable during that time anywhere else. It's still hard for me to believe, when I think back how terrible that night was. Yet all we see is God and his amazing ways of reveling himself. I can honestly say not one of those days went by without us seeing His work. It truly was a spiritual experience for everyone involved.

From the time we pulled up to that awful sight, it was one act of kindness after another. The firemen's efforts, the Red Cross, family, friends and neighbors all helped us while the fire was still burning. Bright and early the very next morning, people began pulling in the driveway to bring their support to us. As I said before, angels came to us in flocks and they kept coming for days.

The first morning we had to meet the fire marshal to determine the cause of the fire. I remember praying that it had nothing to do with anything my wife had done. I know how she is, and she had already been way too hard on herself. He went in alone for about twenty minutes and then asked me to come in so he could show me what he had found. It was very interesting to watch him start at the ceiling and work down lines of different levels of damage. He showed me how the lines pointed down to a floor lamp that had shorted out where the wire went into the base. It didn't make our home situation any better but it sure took a load off my wife's mind. That was the first thing we did that morning, and even it turned out to be a blessing. Just like everything else in life, it can always be worse.

As he climbed back into his vehicle he said, "Well, I guess it's all yours." I remember looking back at the house and thinking just how little all yours amounted to. That's when we entered the house for the first time and started digging through the ashes for anything we might be able to salvage. Talk about a wild ride on an emotional rollercoaster. We would find a keepsake and treasure it for a moment then turn around and find something that could never be replaced. Very little was salvageable. For the most part the house and everything in it was a total loss.

It began to rain about ten o'clock and we had to seek refuge under our front porch. It was the only portion of our former home that still had a roof over it. Try to imagine this picture. We were standing in front of our burned out home. We are covered from head to toe in ashes. It was pouring down rain, and we were standing in the only place there was to stay dry. Since we had made the news that night, a steady stream of cars drove past examining the damage. What some might see as too much to bare or pitiful and sad, we were actually standing there counting our blessings. I bet none of the people who passed at that time could have imagined that would be what we were doing. I was there, and I still have a hard time believing that is what we were doing. Not only were we thankful to still have each other, but we were standing there being thankful we still had a porch to get out of the rain. God has always been a part of our lives and I am very thankful for that. I don't think we could have come out of that the way we did had it not been for our strong faith in Him. I know for a fact, there is no way we could have felt blessed during that time without God. The fact is, it was God's love that sent all those angels flocking to us in our time of need. When the rain stopped, we finished loading stuff out of our garage and headed back to Mom and Dad's.

My wife went into the house as I drove out to the barn to unload the truck. As I went to back up to the barn door the transmission went out of my truck. I was out there by myself and all I could think about was, *how I am going to tell her this one*. They say when it rains it pours, and we were sure getting a good taste of that. Now, instead of just backing the truck into the barn and leaving it for morning I had to unload everything. I took my time because I no longer was in a hurry to get inside. When I sat down at the dinner table it was easy to see the hurt in everyone's eyes. I didn't have the heart to drop another bomb on my family at that time, so I kept that information to myself. I went to bed that night trying to figure out a way I could solve this problem without worrying them. Instead of worrying about the truck, we focused on all the people who had been out that day to help us. It made for a lot better conversation. Thinking about how our family handled the whole situation makes me very proud of all of them.

Our kids had lost everything they had ever owned, and not one time do I remember either one of them complaining about what they didn't have. They would bring up things they lost but not in a way to be pitied. I know it was just as hard for them as it was us. You would have never known what they were going through by their actions. They behaved better than most adults would in a situation like this. That too was a blessing from God. I can't stress how proud I am of both of them. It's hard to believe, but they are even more mature and kind hearted today as they were then.

The weeks that followed were harder for me than the night of the fire. I couldn't get over the never ending acts of kindness that kept showing up at our door. It started bringing tears to my eyes every time someone would show up. It got so bad my wife started referring to me as the big homeless crybaby. It was very touching to all of us. There were so many different people doing so many different things, it started making me feel needy. I did not like that at all. It was important more than ever to me to get in a home of our own. Not so much for our sake, I just didn't want people feeling sorry for us. I knew, as long as we were homeless people, we were going to feel that way. It became more important to me than ever to get back where we were seen as strong, not weak.

I can't list all the acts of kindness that took place that period of time we were at Mom and Dad's. It would be another whole book. Just listing the names of the people who helped us would fill another book. I know some people don't believe in God. I will tell you right now, you can't live the life I've seen and not believe. I couldn't deny the examples of Him I have seen if I wanted to. You might read these words and see me as some kind of bible pusher, but I'm not. I just know what I know and believe what I believe. When I don't have the answers I have always turned to his words, and they have always gotten me through.

I will try to give you an idea what those three weeks were like by telling this one story. My eight-year-old cousin was the same age as our daughter. He came to his mom one night and asked her if he could take some money out of his savings account. She said she was quite surprised because he was proud of his account and had never asked to make a withdrawal. She told him he knew he was supposed to save that and she wanted to know why all of a sudden he would want to take some of his money out.

Without batting an eye, he said, "It's not for me mom." He wanted to buy our daughter a new hamster. He told her he knew how upset she was and he thought if he got her a new one it might make her feel better. He didn't think he would need that money anyway because he had been getting by just fine without it. It is an amazing thing when you can see that much Godly behavior, kindness and love in an eight year old. It says a lot more about the people raising him. There really is only one common denominator in all those people and all those stories. It's the love that has been passed down through generations from a true, believing and knowing God. Imagine that this story is only one of hundreds and you may begin to understand the things we witnessed. You might even be lucky enough to understand how we could be so grateful during such difficult times.

To me it's as simple as three little words with power and meaning so big. God is love. These three words don't mean anything to some people while meaning everything to others. For me, it has been easy to believe, because I've had so many examples in my life. In time, all those examples have brought me to a place in my life where I feel like I know. When you know, it's not about having to believe. It just is believing. I know it's that hard to see all the signs, but I think it's more about how you interpret what you see and what you are looking for when you look. We know attitude affects everything we do. Then we should know our attitude while we look will directly affect what we see. I do know, when we lose a bad attitude it becomes a lot easier to see the good things in life. I hope everyone can come to know. The more you see the better you will get at it. It's like it is multiplied, with one act inspiring many others.

Now its ten years later and I look at where we are thinking what a blessing in disguise that was. My wife and I say all the time, everything happens for a reason. Even things that seem horrible at the time can lead us down a path to a new place or a new understanding for the better. It is so much nicer where we are now compared to where we were then. We have a nice place out in the country that really does feel like home now, but we don't refer to it as our home only. It belongs to our friends and family. We know without each and everyone of them we wouldn't be here. My family is so grateful for everyone who helped us that we vowed to keep our door open to all the rest of our days. We enjoy nothing more than being here with those friends as often as possible. Life really is about the people we have in our life that touch our hearts as well as the people and the hearts we can touch. We will spend the rest of our lives trying to pass on all the love that came to us just through that one experience, let alone all the other reasons we have to do so in our life.

So if you ever wonder how someone can believe so much just think of this story. You can think of the family that was knocked flat on their back in an instant. Before the first pain had time to sink in, the angels came in flocks. Not only would they not allow us to be knocked down, they wouldn't even leave us on one knee. They didn't rest until they had us back up on our feet and knew we could manage on our own again. My family will never forget what we witnessed. We will never doubt the power of God's love. I know we will never forget the night God sent us his angels in flocks and how they scooped us up and flew us to safety out of the fire.

GRANDPA

Four O'clock on Sunday morning,
His truck went down the road.
So others would be nice and warm
while faith lightened their load.
Elder in the Baptist church,
the one his family built.
Shovel snow and stoke the fire,
see the flowers didn't wilt.
He loved God in such a way,
gave his life to the church.
Gave his time to make things right
So all could come in search.
You could see and hear God working
Through him every single day.
He'd sit there and twirl his hair
And watch the children play.
When he sat at the organ
Beautiful music began to flow.
That always made him happy.
You could see him glow.
Violin, piano, organ he would play,
Couldn't read a single note.
Played by ear for all to hear,
Songs for God the people wrote.
I had to learn at thirteen
To drive a stick shift,
Just incase to the hospital
He might need a lift.
A carpenter for all his life,
How much like Jesus can one be?
I never heard him command,
Life is up to you and me.

Never heard a single word,
Talk of others was not right.
Do your job, mind your own
And say a prayer each night.
You'd rarely hear him speak,
But listen you should do.
Every single time he spoke,
Every single word was true.
Fourteen brothers and sisters,
That's how many Grandpa had.
A family farm working together
Back then times were really bad.
I think that's where he came to be
Sufficient in every single way.
The summer months you'd find him
In his garden most everyday,
Planting seeds and hoeing weeds
Fulfilling every family need.
He cared, shared and nourished us
Like God we all agreed
After all the past years
And all the men I've known,
He helped teach me to grow
The way that I have grown.
I see his image all the time
I see him in my dad.

I see him in me more and more,
Grateful that makes me glad.
I know when I look back
What impresses me the most.
There's not a single time I recall
Of himself I never heard him boast.
If you never saw him do
Or no one told you of,
No one would have known
How full he was with love.
This is so very little said

Of a man who taught me to care.
He taught generations of family
How important it is to share.
I want it to be known by all
That such a man was here.
Make him a promise I will keep
Of this I have no fear.
My little girl has given me
My very first granddaughter
In the end, what he taught me
I hope she'd say I taught her.
I hope she see's me like I saw him
Long after I've departed.
And carry on through her grandkids
The love in me he started.
When she remembers me,
I hope she has good thoughts.
Good memories and blessings—
I want to leave her lots.
I hope she remembers me
Like I remember him: in awe.
I hope she smiles the way I do
Just remembering Grandpa.

GOD TOLD ME

God told me I should live
God told me I should give
God told me I should care
God told me I should share
God told me I should seek
God told me I should speak
God told me I should try
God told me I should fly
God told me I should mix
God told me I should fix
God told me I should see
God told me I should be
God told me I should pray
God told me I should play
God told me I should hope
God told me I should cope
God told me I should smell
God told me I should tell
God told me I should hear
God told me I should cheer
God told me I should feel
God told me I should deal
God told me I should earn
God told me I should learn
God told me I should touch
God told me I should clutch
God told me I should find
God told me I should bind
God told me I should know
God told me I should grow
God told me I should tide
God told me I should ride
God told me I should of
God told me I should love

NOTHING TO PROVE

This man has no desire to climb a mountain.
Search for my youth in some long lost fountain.
No reason for this man to jump from a plane.
You have so much to lose and nothing to gain.
Why does any man feel the need to tempt fate?
We're all born with an unknown expiration date.
The lion tamer, I can only wonder what for.
Lions would prefer to stay wild I'm pretty sure.
Thankful I've escaped the addiction for speed.
Things go by blurry seeing clearly difficult indeed.
Some go as far as Russian roulette.
Misguided and lost that's a safe bet.
When given the choice why choose no net.
That's one decision one may live to regret.
Maybe the worst are the ones driven by greed.
Consumed by possessions, that grew from bad seed.
I hear from many their caught up in a rat race.
Is your hurry of need or just more thrills you chase.
Thankful for all things God brought into my life.
Beautiful, healthy children, and an amazing wife.
It was his love that got me through early years.
Not enough knowledge to have any fears.
It was his love that showed me life's thrills
Things that amaze, leave us standing in chills.
Don't think I don't know what I'm talking about.
I've tried many things just to try to figure it out.
I gladly traded sports, travel, fortune and fame,
for thrills in my home and the real rewards came.
To learn more of people than just their name.
It's our lion in us we need to tame.
I learned what I seek is not out there somewhere.
I found the whole time it was waiting right here.

Here in my home family and friends around.
Everything I've ever sought, right here has been found.
Alive and amazed, laughter and joy by the minute.
That is my life with my granddaughter in it.
I've never felt my life to fall so free.
Bring so much peace to my friends and me.
As I said before, I have nothing to prove.
My efforts are shifting starting to move.
God showed me the way. That's one thing I know.
The only thing to prove now, I want to show.
What means most to me, number one on my list?
To those who have doubt, prove God's love exists.
There's no time to waste, there's too much to do.
So many today have their doubts about what is true.
The mission at hand is too important to wait.
For all there's a path leading to an open gate.
Lord help them see. Alone I can't get through.
The words don't come from me, they are coming from you.

THE LOST

I try to seek and find the lost everyday everywhere.
They all have different demons feeding their life's despair.
Without knowing your love they have no light around.
When they try to seek the darkness keeps them bound.
Some struggling with lies, others it's an addiction.
For some loneliness and pain or believing in fiction.
Some were never loved, while others are just spoiled.
Some want to hate, strike like a snake lying coiled.
A few turned their back on God. Now their life gets worse.
While some retreat within, others stand up and course.
Most led astray unknowing, while others leave by choice.
God speaks to them, they choose not to hear his voice.
Excuses they have many, why they were left behind.
Rarely ever seeking you it's no wonder they can't find.
Some say they must see you, they show no faith or trust.
I've seen some go as far as to say you're unjust.
It really doesn't matter how they got where they are.
Without finding you I know they won't go far.
It's up to us all to take that first big leap.
Don't waste one more minute, start before you fall a sleep.
I wonder just how many simply don't know how to pray.
Just send you a list you can do for them today.
Prayers shouldn't be selfish or demand things absurd.
Whining and complaining some say they weren't heard.
God hears every prayer and he knows what is right.
Sometimes he helps us when he just sits there tight.
It seems everyday the lost numbers are growing.
That tugs at the heart of the one who is all knowing.
The way to turn it around and let your new life start.
Help him with his goal he'll speak to your heart.
Will you help him first, no matter what the cost?
He'll bring love to you if you help him save the lost.

Short Quotes

Selfishness is the first step down the path to loneliness.

Sometimes the biggest mistakes are made with the greatest intentions. (Don't stop trying!)

If you think you are better than someone else, it proves you aren't.

If you see your cup as half empty then I bet that's all you see when you look. If you see your cup as half full then I bet you see more than some. If you see your cup as running over I bet you know God. If you see your cup as empty I'll bet you knocked it over with bad choices.

I love happy people. I love trying to create them.

True love is being happiest together!

We can stop fighting and laugh about it if we both choose to do so.

If you cry, you need to toughen up. If you're tough you need to lighten up. If you're at home you should be at work. If you're at work your never home . . . Starting to get it gentlemen?

Saying I do shouldn't mean I have to do everything.

The people always asking you to do stuff can do it themselves, they just don't want to.

No one knows what is best for you. If you don't know for yourself, only God will have the answers.

If you have something better for me to do just say so. (I said better for me, not better for you.)

God's beauty is hard to miss. It's everywhere you look.

Life is lived to the fullest with lots of smiles and laughter.

Maybe I'm not an underachiever. Maybe I was just over rated.

Approach marriage like a life sentence and always keep in mind you have to sleep with the warden.

If you don't like disappointment maybe I should apologize before we get started.

If wanting more makes me selfish, well I guess just call me selfish.

Women should be treated with respect even if the ones who bring it to your attention the most deserve it the least.

I watched a show on how to increase your memory, but I forgot what they said to do.

No one has to be judgmental and condescending. They all choose to be.

Odds are if any of these make you feel uncomfortable, it's because they hit to close to home.

The grass may not be any greener on the other side of the fence, but you sure have a pretty yard.

For a lot of men it's not a matter of lack of knowledge and concern. It's a lack of respect and control.

In the world of wisdom, I wonder if this would be a misprint.

Most people take themselves too seriously. If you don't believe me, just ask them something and listen.

Don't discourage your children. They will fly a lot higher when you get out of their way.

Take pride in your life, your look and your actions. You are unique and beautiful just the way you are. The world needs the love you possess inside.

Life isn't that stressful with God. Trying to live it without him can be hell on earth.

Why would you expect your kids to be saints when they grew up listening to you tell your friends how messed up you are.

Maybe it's not his truth or my truth you are afraid of. Maybe it's your truth that has you avoiding truth all together.

A clear mind is capable of doing great things from a wheelchair. A clouded one has trouble functioning with a healthy body under it.

Answer to ancient question; if a tree falls in the woods and no one is there to hear it, does it still make a sound? Of course it does! You really do think it is all about you don't you?

People ask me when I plan to grow up. I don't know! I hadn't planned on it.

While you stop to smell the roses keep in mind you still have to watch for bees.

All churches don't want you to know all things. God does!

There are two sides to every story. I'm not sure either one of these are right.

Don't take their word for it. Take God's!

Saying you don't believe in God or the Devil is like saying you've never seen the effects and don't know the difference between good and evil.

Some people want to be lied to because the truth about them is too much for them to deal with.

Men and women have no problem getting along. Boys and girls do. (Age is irrelevant)

There are two ways to look at life. Live it or watch it go by.

People who write are always talking about the bestseller list. The number one bestseller is the bible. It always has been and always will be.

How I See Women

How to put thoughts, feelings and emotions in poem
How to find the right words so important to show them
Not every man gazes your way with ill intent
Some just thanking God for what heaven has sent
I understand why you're all poised for attack
Most stares are at body parts when you turn your back
Though it may be uncommon even considered quite rare
This man see's so much more than just the color of hair
It's not always demeaning something sexual all the time
No need for mace or police, no intention of crime
I'm going to try my best to share my personal view
Why you should see yourself the way I look at you
I see God's greatest work, his own living art
From your head to your toes in the depths of your heart
There is a reason why he saved you for last in creation
Everything had to be perfect for such an amazing elation
He knew from the start you would all be his treasure
Gave you all of his gifts, way too many to measure
Every man who knows God will tell you this too
You can't come to know God without his sight in you
He didn't ask what I thought, actually he commanded
Special attention to you, not requested but demanded
This man looks at you proud of the thoughts in his head
Don't misunderstand and stop wishing we all drop dead
I see care in your eyes and light in your smile
Love in your kind heart and still all the while
You think I should look away, you think nothing to see
While I'm seeing God's greatest work standing before me
God's living artwork growing and changing everyday
You wouldn't dare say to God but a good man look away
God knows my heart knows my thoughts are all true
Like the sunrise, stars and mountains I look at you

The eyes of the artist see the beauty in almost all things
You could be in museums like the greatest paintings
It's sad without knowing me, you think you're disrespected
My respect for you and God only by you undetected
I'm failing him when I fail to see all his beauty
I can see him in your face, not just some little cutie
Next time you look up and catch a man starring
Take time to find out if he's undressing or caring
So many disappointments, I know you've heard many lies
But some men are looking at you through God's eyes
I won't pretend not to notice the beauty of your skin
How dare you assume I'd stop there not looking within
I know the beauty I'm seeing is of no certain age
Not your height or your weight do my eyes engage
All five of my senses, nothing pleases so much
Sight, sound, smell, taste and you know even your touch
Every man's a king and benefits from your existence
Knowing all that you are, he will travel any distance
I'm amazed at the power hidden in your attention
Take your love away a man is like nothing I will mention
If I could sit down with every woman on earth
I would say whatever it is can be seen at your birth
I would ask you to relax, stretch out and take comfort
Take a look at yourself; take a break from all effort
You can't save the world although most of you try
Moving at warp speed to answer everyone's cry
It's your very well being you placed last on your list
I'd ask you to place yourself first and I'd have to insist
You're first on my list and that is the truth
Do us both a favor, don't forget the girl in your youth
Back when you laughed, dreamed and still gave to yourself
That girls still alive just been placed on a shelf
Spend time with you eager to hear every word
Knowing that when you speak an angel is heard
Just basking in your presence a man feels complete
So many deserving to have oil rubbed on their feet
I love every woman, without disrespecting my wife
She sees the same when she looks at your life

We both have been blessed by the true love of God
If you don't see what I see maybe it's you that's odd
Grandmas, mothers, daughters, sisters, wives and more
Love comes from you all, it flows from every pore
Many men misguided, only see what you can do for him
To me your very presence is way too good for them
That presence is a blessing, God's most cherished gift
You fix the hearts of others while your own needs a lift
God told me to watch close and never turn away
To cherish and admire you, I do this more every day
How else could I have possibly ever come to know
The awesome things in you he wanted to show
You see me look at you and you think you're so fine
Know I see grandma and grandbaby just as Devine
Some think for looking I should have something to say
I'm just watching God work before me every day
While I've got your attention, tell you while I can
Watching you live your life made me a better man

THE CHASE

I've chased the fowl all my days
Eyes to the sky just sit and gaze
Corn fed Canada's in Illinois
My father taught me there was joy
Early morning mallards fall from the skies
Stirring the soul through eager eyes
Bluebills, redheads, ringneck, canvasback
Like a big water fighter jet attack
Large flocks swooping on wings that roar
Blink once and they're there no more
Same thing with teal twisting and turning
Maximum fuel their jet engines burning
Serenade on the creek bank cry of a woodie
Gone with the ice break out the hoodie
Pintails and widgeon the wary gadwall
Traveled the nation in search of them all
North Dakota October clouds of snow geese
Flock after flock, seem never to cease
Arkansas rice fields, mallards galore
Green timber flooded find even more
Been down to the Texas Gulf shore
So many pintails and widgeon our arms got sore
Alberta, Saskatchewan and even Manitoba
Three provinces we hunted in Canada
Every day not about the birds alone
All God's creation to all of us shown
The people the places in my mind right now
Passing like ships in chase of the fowl
Southeast Missouri over into Kentucky
Two places we've been more than just lucky
Southwest Indiana, Reelfoot lake Tennessee
All places the waterfowl can always fly free

142

Where or what everyday there's no guarantee
Just a beautiful day made for you and me
Up, out and ready before the daylight
Sit there and wait until dark of night
Cold, wind, rain, snow mixed with sleet
Break up the ice just to warm your feet
Creeks, lakes and swamps in the sunrise
Go there and you will leave there quite wise
Created by him everything in view
Every single day is glorious and new
Not seeing at all what most call the sights
Out in the fields just waiting for flights
Gear packed and ready waiting for the call
Phone rings more when the season is fall
Miles of highway between place to place
For those of us caught in the waterfowl chase

EVELYNN

Let me tell you about a woman I know
Always helping others, always on the go
Steady as a rock for her family
A sweet living angel, everyone can see
God in her life, love in her heart
Working for together, never for apart
Most of her life a loving caring nurse
Something from inside, something you can't rehearse
Teaching all others how they can give
Showing better ways we all can live
Teaching generations what, where and why
And everything we do deserves our best try
Proud of the fact her door's always open
Live more like her that's what I'm hopin'
When it comes to family all know she'll be there
Answers to the problem always glad to share
I know many people love her very much
For the many ways their heart she did touch
If you choose to sit, to her words just listen
You can find the things your heart has been missin'
Her house full of love, seen when you walk in
Best take her advice if you choose to win
As far as people go she has all my respect
God's angel here on Earth is what I detect
The only thing I know that drives her up the walls
Year and year again rake them darn gumballs
One thing I know for sure, I've known it for a while
Think of how she lives, it will make you smile
Gather all today, her birthday it is here
Celebrate a life, one that makes us cheer
Ninety years today doing just for others
Always standing out when it comes to mothers
You'll see God today, look straight into heaven
When you stare in the eyes of the angel they call Evelynn

WE DON'T KNOW

Have you ever had something you hated?
Years down the road it made you elated
What about the one you used to despise
Down on your luck they came to your cries
Dread facing the music all day long
To find out it was the most beautiful song
No way to know what's best for our self
Place the urge to tell others back on the shelf
All the time wishing you could be older
Now that you are, your feet just get colder
Waiting forever for a date just with them
That day finally comes but the spark was dim
All time is wasted, just waiting to know
Just dive in the river and ride in its flow
What comes our way is what He meant
For you to grow stronger its heaven sent
When you get off and pick your own path
Don't blame another, you caused the wrath
You might miss out around the next bend
Don't get off course, let Him be your friend
Wait until you retire and then enjoy
Weeks later it's over, a cemetery convoy
You will think things that now you don't
Be careful of times you swear that you won't
I've seen this in my life time after time
Fail to see it in your own to yourself do a crime
We let our own minds limit our options
When limiting those proceed with all cautions
Roll with the punches nothing is planned
With options all open the flame is fanned
Keep the fire burning that's everyone's goal
Ideas as different as sun, wind, gas or coal

You look in the mirror and see only the flaws
The rest see your beauty not a monster with claws
Thought you wouldn't like it so you didn't go
Chose to stay home ten years in a row
Finally you decided it was time for a change
Time of your life how's that for strange
How many times did you say you're on your own?
Now you're sitting there and you're all alone
Help this person the thought you embrace
Then your best effort blows up in your face
All the worlds' knowledge and your best insight
Only God knows for all what's wrong and what's right

INSIDE

We search our whole life through
To find out what is true
A need for something new
Look for answers what we do
To satisfy our mind
Those answers we must find
No time to unwind
Its life you can't rewind
It's like we lost the key
Understanding you and me
We're only really free
When we can simply be
You won't find it in cars
Or way out past the stars
No need to look on mars
For life is truly ours
God is all we need
Our souls He will feed
When cut we all bleed
We're all of the same creed
Simply look within
Then you will begin
A life that has no sin
The only way to win
Don't have to look outside
Or take another ride
The answers they can't hide
You have them all inside

ALEIGHA

May 31ˢᵗ the year 2010
A brand new life is to begin
The first day you made me smile
You've touched my heart all the while
You brought me joy from the start
Everyday you touch my heart
Can't believe how time goes by
You make me smile and I know why
My love for you will never weaken
Trust these words to you I'm speakin'
I cherish every single minute
Thankful my life has you in it
Unable to speak or read and write
So for now I will just hold on tight
Someday you'll understand these words
And remember we sat and watched the birds
I give you this poem from Grandpa
Still waiting to hear "Hey PaPa"
I hope that you will understand
The love I feel when you hold my hand
Today we honor your first year
These words for you a special cheer
You teach me as much as I teach you
I enjoy watching everything you do
Living, loving, laughing when you're around
My greatest joy in you I've found
My feelings for you come from up above
Thanks for bringing me so much love!

Love always PaPa!

THE FIFTIETH

Fifty years have come and gone
A love that seems to carry on
Many years now have passed by
Natural love, don't have to try
Two as one we all can see
Teaches all how love should be
Sharing life and all it brings
To our hearts your love sings
Some of us would not know life
Without you two as husband and wife
From today back to the start
Love held deep in each heart
All can see your love is true
It shows in everything that you do
Three strong kids that grow not wilt
From the house that you two built
Love so special and so divine
Time to gather and share some wine
All those gathered are here to say
This is truly a special day
You showed us all the way to live
To us all your love you give
To you both we make a toast
To know your love we all boast
Thanks so much, you touched us all
Love's the strength so we don't fall
To celebrate this special time
I write for you this little rhyme
Not just your love that makes me glad
You see, I can call you Mom and Dad

Love lives forever!

Short Quotes

They said they couldn't get the halo to fit over the horns

Your nose may not be growing, but the distance between you and God is

Tell the truth and it will set you free. Stick to your story and it will stick with you too

Don't turn out your lights when you know eventually they will go out on their own

Living life to the fullest isn't meal to meal

I know God provided it. You must have lost or spilled it

I can't tell you the answer only where to look

Time is like the wind. You don't see it but it is blowing by

Don't cry to me. Pray to him!

I told him I didn't think I could love you. He said go back and try again.

God doesn't make mistakes, but He sure makes a lot of people that do.

I thought I was about done. He said write some more!

I thought this was going on forever. Then I thought about how long He has been doing it.

I chose to walk with God. I feel like I get it right when I only see one set of footprints. I follow Him and try to walk in His footsteps.

I don't know everything, but I know it wasn't God that told you to turn your back on them.

Don't sit in loneliness when you can search for happiness

Don't waste time trying to cheer someone up who chose to be unhappy.

You don't need someone else's encouragement. Take what he gave you and encourage yourself.

I never read about the whiners in God's army.

First I wondered, then I believed, now I know.

Just as God and good are real so are the Devil and evil. The more you try to do God's work the more the Devil will attack you and your efforts. The good news is God always wins and now you see where the Devil was coming from.

I know people will attack even these simple well-intended words. We're taking names.

If anyone feels threatened by these simple words, maybe they should.

The time is now! Can't you see the angels falling all around you?

Save a dollar and live another day. Save a life and live for an eternity.

It is adult hide and seek. You see him then something happens and you can't. Seek and find him again as something else tries to steal your faith.

Bridges can take years to build, minutes to destroy and some can never be rebuilt.

I like to think Jesus and I could have watched the sunset over bread and wine with a mutual respect for each other.

If you want to know and feel love, then give it.

God gave you your kids, now you can give them even more. Give your kids God.

The letter 't' alone is just a letter, but it's powerful enough to keep you from your dreams if you add it to can.

If He didn't do it for you then maybe He is waiting for you to see you can do it for yourself.

God is in everything especially love.

If you're not happy then you haven't found Him, even if you thought you did.

TIME

Time is the treasure, not silver or gold.
Years only few or will you grow old.
How will you spend the time he is giving?
Sit and watch others or go out and start living
Will you make the most of each passing day,
Or wait for tomorrow while today slips away?
Each day is a gift. Reach out and take it.
You live how you choose, don't choose to fake it.
Blink of an eye life's here and gone.
Pray that you see the next day to dawn.
Everywhere everyday opportunities are there.
Smiles with another, what better to share?
We all get knocked down or stop to ask why.
Time just won't wait, it will pass you by.
Marching like a soldier, time keeps the pace.
Why people feel the need to hurry or race.
Sometimes it's best spent doing nothing at all.
Clear off that calendar that hangs on the wall.
Sometimes our days, our time spent very wise.
Sit with loved ones and enjoy the sunrise.
The world is a stage and you are the star.
Your performance will last as long as you are.
How many hearts will you touch with your time?
Could you have touched more I'll bet my last dime.
How much time of ourselves do we boast?
When listening to others is what matters most.
Time is of value not a minute to waste.
How do I spend it decide not in haste
I promise your wealth will not by a minute.
You're running a race and you'll never win it.
When it comes to time you have one way to win.
You spend most of it spreading love from within.
The one thing they put on every headstone—
The time you were here—not possessions you owned.

CHOSEN ROAD

A different road we all must choose
Life is short with no time to lose
Pick the road your life will go down
Lead us to a smile, away from a frown
Don't drive to slow or go to fast
Steer away from trouble to make it last
Turns and curves, stoplights along the way
Before you hit the gas I want to say
Ask all you can who's been down that road
Was it worth the trip, listen to what you're told
Don't waste your gas or the time in your life
Down any road that just leads to strife
Look for the roads that bring you joy
Ones with few people who intend to annoy
Some may be crowded, others less traveled
A relaxing drive, confusion unraveled
In our youth we all drive much faster
We need to slow down to avoid a disaster
Me, I suggest the roads that you drive
The ones that make you feel most alive
I like to travel down different paths
Changes our minds like clothes after baths
The only way that we get to see
All of the gifts he left you and me
As I grow older I slow down the ride
Try to take it all in his way I abide
Highways and streets are not all I speak
A dirt road, a trail or path by a creek
I hope in your life your road is smooth
Peace in your heart and mind just to sooth
On foot or horseback, on bikes or in cars
In light of day or under the stars

Your roads traveled, they go by in a flash
Hope to see the last mile, avoid the big crash
So many things for you to behold
Driving to him on your chosen road

THE COWBOY

Imagine a heart that's untamed and wild
A need to be free felt since a child
Sleep with the stars, up with the sun
Life, death and justice in the barrel of a gun
A man who stands alone before his maker
The goal everyday, cheat the undertaker
Mind, back and hands are tools to survive
At home in the wild he feels so alive
Nothing as great as bringing in the herd
Strength, truth and God spoke in each word
He's living the life that God intended
No man rests until all fences mended
Hard to understand a man so solitary
Loves time with God, people make him wary
Unable to be free in big city life
Office's, desks and ties cause this man strife
Free as the wind and the wild mustang
If you don't understand, he don't give a dang
They think he's searching or why would he roam
You should understand, everywhere is his home
He lives with God in the almighty's house
No fear to live, he won't hide like a mouse
How much more in your life would you do?
If you found the cowboy living in you
Would you sit taller up in the saddle?
Choose to do right no need for a paddle
Be true to yourself when living each day
When you are alone take time to pray
Take care of the land daylight to dark
Fire in your eyes for life there's a spark
Hold your life on a straight narrow course
Before you rest would you care for your horse?

He's going the way of the great dinosaur
Cowboys are few, not many any more
Set your life free then ride like the wind
Enjoy who you are and be your best friend
Riding life's trails will bring you great joy
Releasing in you that long lost cowboy

HUGS

Sweet embrace means so much
Heart to heart when we touch
Heaven at work as we clutch
For a lame heart it is the crutch

Warms our heart when we feel
Love wrapped around is so real
For the hungry heart it is a meal
Care for another that's the deal

Hold on tight the heart will glow
Love inside to help us all grow
From one to another it will flow
Power in each that's all I know

A loving touch that we all need
Not the stomach, the heart we feed
A gift of love it plants the seed
Another's garden we help to weed

Means so much to get it right
Don't let go hold on tight
One for your kids every night
I tell you it's a beautiful sight

Once you start soon you will see
No greater comfort for you or me
Worries all gone and love set free
It's Gods way, the only way to be

I suggest right now you start
You will feel another's heart
How you find more in your cart
Hearts together instead of apart

I have known for quite a while
Every hug will bring a smile
Mark it down, put it on file
You'll get more out of every mile

It's like honey from a bee
Looked upon its love you see
God's love you are setting free
Bond of hearts of you and me

Short Quotes

Anyone can see the beauty of an angel. To know the heart and mind of one is the true treasure.

You see the way you look!

Remember yesterday, live today and pray for tomorrow.

Believe, trust, seek, find then live. Best results in that order.

Don't run! Kneel!

Find God anywhere you look. He's everywhere!

God's words are right! Man's interpretation is usually wrong.

Finding the truth is not going to be enough if you are not going to believe it or live it.

See how the ones who deny His love like to cling to their weaknesses.

I know you don't think you need to read these simple words. That tells me that maybe you do.

Are you going to grow or wilt?

Anytime with God is good. Right now is always a good time.

You couldn't wait to tell them they were wrong. Now go back and tell them all the things they do right and all the things you did wrong (don't leave anything out).

Stop fighting, you're wrong! Both of you!

You think you are so much better than everyone. You don't have to prove it. You're wrong and you just did!

If you only read one book in your life make sure it is the right one.

I'm still waiting for someone to explain to me why God is not a mandatory credit to graduate.

If this is one nation under God, tell me how did He get under its feet.

He said to come to Him as a child, not the commander in chief.

Before you waste more time arguing, you should know some people don't mind being wrong.

Throughout history thousands have agreed with his message. How many believe in yours?

I bet He sent you ten different answers and you weren't paying attention all ten times.

He said there seems to be a lot of ADD these days so maybe short quotes will help.

It's your choice: stand like the mighty oak, fall like the leaves or crack like a nut.

God has a sense of humor; He has a sense of everything.

It's OK to cry for a little while.

There's beauty in everything! Why don't you see it?

I'd rather be broke and serve Him than be rich from selling my soul.

What can one man do? Anything with God!

Your ticket is already purchased. Just do it because you know you should not to buy your way in.

Live for others, and He will live for you.

Most of life is just common sense. You don't like to see yourself as common do you?

Friends with wallets often leave you behind. Friends with hearts wouldn't dare.

You can buy friends but they are not cheap. You can borrow friends but only for a while. You can make friends that will last a lifetime.

God gives you what you need. You just want to much!

When you hear Gods words you can't keep them to yourself. If you feel the need to they are not Gods words.

I shout it from the mountain top. I shout it through the valley too.

Amazing Grace; everything in two words

When your time comes they won't come to pay respect for the things you collected. They will come for what you gave and the lives you affected.

Not all laws are Gods laws. As usual some men think they can do better.

Things like this expose the Devil. He will attack and then run from it every time. See there goes another one!

The one person that can, do and will do the most damage to you is you.

Maybe people should stop throwing rocks and crawl back under them.

A mind is a terrible thing to waste. Time is even worse!

I know people who make the most out of the least. I know people who make the least out of the most. What do you think the difference is? I think I know!

I'm no saint. I'm far from perfect. I know that much.

Take time for Him before He takes it back.

It's your life, your heart, your mind, your soul and your body. Do what you want with it. I have to feed mine.

I understand how you feel, because I didn't know either.

I can't believe all the people I meet living in bondage with no chains. Do you think they are locked in their own minds?

You can sell your soul, but you can't buy it back and they are very hard to earn back.

I know you are rubbing me, but I'm just not sure it is the right way.

You think you have a hard time dealing with your kids. You should see what He has to put up with.

I'm not going to say He is not happy with the way things are going, but I will say when I try to look at the world through His eyes it doesn't make me very happy.

THE LIGHT IS NOT BLACK OR WHITE

One might chose to believe that a title like this could only be about race. Nothing could be farther from the truth. Actually this is a story about judgment. I've witnessed a lot of changes in the last few years. Progress has been made in many different areas, and our knowledge has exploded in recent years. We are very fortunate to live in such a time with so many different opportunities waiting before us. Even in economic times like these, people find a way to hold strong to their beliefs and dreams. The overall spirit of the American dream is still alive. It does seem to be under a constant threat. I'm not sure why or even where the true threat is coming from. I do know there is a smoke screen being used against us that is intended to divide us instead of bringing us together. There is one thing that is taking place that really bothers me, and that is the attempt to take us away from God.

With all the knowledge possessed by man in this day and age you would think we would be coming closer together. Instead I watch as we seem to be divided and conquered a little more everyday that goes by. Just as in nature together we are strong. There is strength in numbers. That is something that has been proven over time. I am beginning to think that there is more division coming from within than from outside sources. Who decided we don't need to pray in school or public places anymore? Why aren't the Ten Commandments on every courthouse wall above the constitution? After all, this is still the United States of America the last time I checked. When did we decide to stop acting like it? It wasn't my choice and I haven't talked to very many who say it was theirs. We used to get answers and then use them to solve problems instead of create them. The farther we get from God's words with our modern opinions and laws, the worse our lives have become. At the rate we are going, our kids will never know anything about the true American dream. I write this with the future of our children in mind and the hope that something might change for their sake.

Our forefathers were seemingly, a very intelligent group. You could say they were unspoiled by the corruption of today. At the same time what they were fleeing from was a prime example of what they foresaw in our future. Now if any man can, I would sure appreciate it if he would prove what I am about to say wrong and I will shut up. Our constitution is the law of this land. The original constitution is anyway. I will add that because I'm not sure that all the changes that have been made are even legal, especially the ones that have been made in recent years by people since exposed as thieves or liars. How many people have literally been run out of Washington in just the last decade? The very statement "one nation under God" makes it clear that no law will ever take precedence over God's law. If you ever wondered why there is a group of people trying to remove God from everything, well there you go. As long as that one statement holds true then there are many things that would destroy this country that can never happen.

How many laws written in recent years will stand up in God's court? I'm glad my name isn't on a lot of those laws. Every last law created by mankind will be held accountable the man who imposed it by the creator himself. As for me, I choose not to tell any man or woman what they can or can't do. When you read the constitution (the original version) it basically states in every way possible that we are to uphold God's law as well as protect and preserve human rights. There is nothing in the original stating rights are to be taken away, restricted by government or imposed and enforced on another. I think it's ironic that most politicians see their claim to fame as putting their name on a new law and seeing their will written in the book. I would rather use my name to get rid of some of the ridiculous ones that are on the book right now. There would be a sense of pride that way and I wouldn't have to kneel before God and answer for taking another mans freedom.

Where did all the answers go? Really! Nobody has an answer anymore. When did everything come up for debate? The truth is, nothing in the news being debated today is even open for debate. The answers are in the original constitution of this country. And it clearly states to anyone with any degree of intelligence that it is only truly upheld under the word of God. The Supreme Court is not in Washington. The Supreme Court comes from a much higher authority. That is what our forefathers hoped when they collectively, intentionally and proudly placed under God in and above all else written. The Ten Commandments are the laws of God and the laws they intended to preserve with those words. Most true Americans I have met still hold these values to be of the utmost importance.

The title refers to the ridiculous belief that there is a black or white answer for every question. Just as every man's walk with God is different, so is the life He was given and the path he has been led down. I can't believe we have reached a point where someone is constantly trying to enforce their beliefs on another. What happened to each his own and love thy neighbor? If you seek the ultimate life to live, which I believe is what we all do in one way or another, then you have to seek better ways to be human. God's laws are few when you think about it. They can be copied down, studied and learned by a child in a short period of time. More than a list of laws, his words are more a list of suggestions on living a more rewarding life here on earth. Every man, woman and child was given a right to life through him along with a promise to be allowed to live it the way they choose.

There are no petty laws in Gods words. As for me, I think the most focus as well as the most important thing to be taken is about judgment. All men fail when it comes to a perfect record of not judging others. While some rarely fail at this, others never even come close to getting it right. Judgment of another is quickly leading us down the wrong path. We have gotten completely off course, and it started when we decided everything and everyone needed to conform to one way of thinking. Almost every good idea that ever came to be came from someone else. Sharing ideas with people not like us is how we actually grow and learn. Our lives become stagnant when we surround ourselves only with people who think the way we do.

When we try to force someone to agree with us, we are taking away his or her freedom. When we turn our back or argue with them for not agreeing with us, we are judging them for their right to decide for themselves. It doesn't matter what the subject. It doesn't matter how large or small. Just as you have your rights to live your life as you choose to, so do I. No man has the right to take that away from another. One must be free from judgment of another to truly live a life of God's words. Not free from being judged but free from judging another. Knowing we don't have the right to decide for another then why are we being told we must decide on everything for everyone? Why in recent years has there been such an effort to pick a topic and pretend to make a decision one way or the other for everyone to abide by.

The reason for all this indecision despite all the so-called best efforts to make one is as in many cases money. The money is in the fight. You can pick any topic and claim there are two sides, even though in reality there are often many sides to any topic, and there will be someone ready to choose one or the other. That's not a problem. The problem is when anyone of those people decides they have the right to enforce their chosen side on everyone else then we have a problem. Even God doesn't force anyone to live their life anyway other than the way they choose. I don't see where any government or organization elected by me to serve me has the right to tell me how to live my life. The only Godly way to run anything is with freedom of choice to all. It's definitely not freedom of choice by enforcing a law on all. It's like we have turned around and started riding into the sunrise while we still claim to be going west. For someone that comes from a simpler time, it's hard to understand how something so basic and so simple has become so complicated.

Gun control, abortion, marijuana, illegal aliens, adoption, politics, civil rights, racism, sexism, religion and the death penalty are just a few of the issues facing us on a daily basis. I've sat in disbelief for the last few years as the smartest, most capable country in the world stands before all everyday and says we don't know what to do. Since when does this country not know what to do? We are currently being led to behave this way because there is a lot of money in the argument. When there are two sides raising money hand over fist to enforce their wishes, why make a decision? Then the money would stop coming in. We can't have that, so we need to study and delay any current decisions to think this through. Are you kidding me? Your money is being taken and you are handing it over willingly if you are one of the ones sending checks to fight your cause. And just why is that your cause anyway. Shouldn't that money be used to help the needy right in your own backyard?

The truth is, none of the issues listed before are actually issues at all. You see in the United States of America, one nation under God, everyone has the right to freedom of choice for their own life. That's just the way it is. Sorry to all of you that think you have the right to tell others what to do. Actually, you don't have the right to tell another living soul what they must do. I know that doesn't sit well with many in this day and age but it is true. Look it up. I hated history when I was in school. But I have learned over the years that to truly understand anything you have to study the past. To learn how anything came to be, you must trace it back to its origin. Every year we seem to get a little farther away from God's law while man's law imposes itself upon us even more. It's sad that the one thing that separated us from the rest is the same thing we are trying to remove from our heritage. The very thing that made this country great was the very desire to follow God's words to the letter. There even was a time when we were proud of our beliefs and went as far as boasting about them.

What would happen if we went back to His words for guidance? Shouldn't every man have a right to choose his own path? Live and let live. What if no one judged another from this minute forward? Under the constitution, under God I have no right to judge another for their beliefs. They have the right to believe what they choose to believe. All another can do is voice their opinion. All the division comes through us when we choose to judge. We judge people on the color of their skin, their wealth, their possessions, height, weight even the way they wear their hair. It's their hair! What business is it of yours? I don't believe in abortions, but I don't feel I should have the right to force that opinion on another. I believe in guns, but, again, that doesn't give me the right to try to force everyone to own one. Bottom line is you have the right to choose for yourself and you should be thankful for that right. Many men and women have died for that right. Just as you have the right to your belief, so does the person you are fighting with. So stop it. You either can be right or wrong. It really doesn't matter to most of us. Just leave us alone with your desire to tell us we don't have the same rights you do.

What is it that makes us so eager to judge others? For one thing, we are bombarded by people who don't have a clue how to live. They are constantly telling us not to associate with those over there. How many times a day does someone try to convince you to pick a side and fight with them for some amazing cause? I won't single anybody out but some people need to get a grip on their so-called causes. Maybe, instead of taking up another's cause we could just get a life of our own with so much meaning that we don't have so much time on our hands. Every argument stems from the judgment of another for not thinking like we do. It's a mystery to me when throughout our lives things happen to change our way of seeing the world. Often, we find we didn't know what was in our own best interest, let alone someone else's. Everyone involved in a battle right now is wrong. How's that for something to think about? No matter how right you think you are, if you are demanding it of another you are wrong.

How much time would be left for good deeds if everyone went home put their protest signs in the trash where they belong and went out with a smile instead of a fist? Imagine if you, yes you, put down your cause and picked up all that's needed to prepare a meal for the elderly couple

across the street. Maybe play with the single mom's kids while she gets a much-needed break. Believe it or not, there are much more important and meaningful ways to spend your time. I donate to the Red Cross and a couple other well-known organizations. Other than that, there are too many causes right here in our neighborhood that need to be addressed. Nothing is a better cause than bringing people together. That is the best way I have found to determine if any cause is worthy. If it brings people together then it is indeed a good cause. If it is to create opposition and conflict, it may be not so worthy. Ask yourself if your cause is worthy. Before you answer, will you be honest with yourself and think twice. It's harder to see the truth in us sometimes than it is others.

Before I go any farther I want to stress that this is not an attempt to sound anti-American. I love this country and all it stands for. It is still the greatest country in the world. I have the greatest respect for the men and women that put on a uniform and served it. The problem facing this country now is getting back to God's law. There is no problem threatening us today that can't be solved through the thoughts and words in the Holy Bible. Learning to stop passing judgment is the only thing that will fix our problems. Not easy when we are encouraged everyday to judge each other. We are being led to believe that after passing that judgment we should do everything in our power to seek and destroy our new sworn enemy. I watch as people fight over issues like guns, abortion etc. and just shake my head. There is no fight. There are no right sides. Every man has his right to his own choice. To put it bluntly: pick yours and shut up. That might not sound very kind, but the truth of the matter is that it's the only way to have a true walk with God right here on earth.

Imagine if right now, this very minute, everyone decided to accept everyone else for who they choose to be. I think it would be the greatest moment on earth since man first set foot on it. I will be the first to say it is not easy. It is most difficult with the ones we love the most. Even more surprising to me is the fact a lot of judgment actually comes from love. Often an overbearing love but its love just the same. Every person should make themselves aware of their judgmental ways and make it their first priority in every situation they face from this day forward. I tell you right now you won't believe how many times you judge another on any given day. Even more amazing than that is how many times you will witness someone else judging another. It will start to sicken you in time. I've reached a point in my life that I desire spending my time with the people who judge the least. I've found they are always the most God like in every aspect of their life.

We have to learn to see past the differences. It is the only way to grow mentally, spiritually and forgivingly. That is the way this country tackled every problem it faced just a few short years ago. The main thing is it worked. Without Him we are nothing. Look what this country is rapidly becoming as we take God out of school and our court systems. Who wants to stand up and take the credit for that decision? The more I learn and understand about God the harder it gets for me to judge another. I've found I like myself a lot better that way. I have always been fairly tolerant. That had a lot to do with a thirty year successful marriage. I still have a long way to go, but I'm a lot closer than I used to be. The reward from it all for me has been the peace that comes with it. The peace is real because you truly don't mind their different opinion. You're not disappointed by another's decision. What is there to argue about if you don't stick your nose in their business? It is that you know? It's their business. Best when we all mind our own. That's all I know.

Even our own kids are not our possessions to be controlled. The children that go the farthest get the support they need to achieve their goals not ours. The most amazing people I've ever met are no more or no less than just themselves. It truly is a beautiful thing to see someone succeed and remain being who they are at the same time. Our only place in another's life is to be there for support and offer our best knowledge when asked. The when asked part is very important. A lot of people miss that one. When we choose not to judge, we are accepting of everyone, more tolerant of others and a calmer, gentler human being. We all like being around people like that. Don't you want people to like being around you? That's all it takes. No whining about another, no back stabbing, no complaints, no worries, no breakdowns and no wasted time. That last one is a big one. Time here is short and there really is not a minute to waste. Speak of the things and the ones you love instead of the other option.

How much money would be saved on studies, debates, committees, organizations, court battles, legal fees, protests, marches, crime, vandalism, big government, advertising and politicking if all were under God's law of man's freewill? Where would the argument be then? Want a gun? Get one. If you don't want to own a gun then just don't. The same principle works for all the before mentioned arguments. What is happening now is we are catering to the offended. They have no right to be offended in the first place. The offended judge others, which is the only way to become offended in the first place. The more I learn, the more I know passing judgment is one of the worst offences in God's eyes. It is one of the few things repeatedly spoken over and over again.

One of the biggest reasons for the decline in trust in organized religion is the lack of acceptance and tolerance for all. Only a true hypocrite can say they are of God and at the same time say they refuse to recognize another person or religion. As I search for a life with less judgment and begin to tolerate all people, I realize I am only now beginning to experience real freedom. The word "freedom" plays such an important roll in all of this. Freedom is the greatest thing any man or woman can experience. True freedom is the hope and dream of all civilized men and women. Many have died for it. It is something no one should ever take for granted. It is one of the few things in this world worth fighting or dying for. Any other reason would be in vain. The only other reason that comes to mind is self-defense. When a life is taken for one of these two reasons, it is understandable under God's law and even spoken with words an eye for an eye.

Are we really fighting a cause that's worthy, or are we just looking for a fight. I know for a fact that in some cases it is just someone looking for one. God knew that judgment would be the downfall of mankind, and that is why it was expressed so often in his words. I have found the older and wiser I get that no one can truly even know freedom when they are judgmental. There is a constant feeling of disappointment and frustration that comes with the thought another won't accept your way as the only way. When we are judgmental, we have a harder time realizing the positive things about people and tend to start focusing on the negative. When you really get into the way people interact with one another and the way they develop their attitudes towards one another, you start to see how judgment affects every aspect of our life. Those raised by those who judge will for sure grow up judging others. The reason why the problem seems to get worse is because it is. Even those raised by those who don't judge have a tendency to grow up judging others. It is basic human nature to see ourselves as doing everything the best way possible. Naturally, anyone who doesn't do it our way we feel the need to judge as wrong. Bottom line is it's easy to see how easy it is to judge another. It's just as easy to see how hard it is not to judge another.

Although it may be difficult it is not impossible. That is why I said earlier it is something you have to remain constantly aware of if you wish to discover true freedom. Everyone of us can think of many times we didn't know what was best for our own good. What would make any of us think we know what is best for anyone else? It runs over into our attempt to raise kids. We see the opportunity to steer them in the direction we think they should go. It is easy to forget they are not us and that they have their own personal relationship with God to contend with. Even as parents, we only have the right to suggest a path, not force it. We can force it but that doesn't mean we have a right to. When the creator expects us to stray off the right path at times, he has never forsaken or not forgiven anyone who has done so. That is the very basis of his words and what the whole deal is based on. He knows we will fall short at times. We know we will fall short at times. Why do we tend to look upon others and fail to see our own faults as we pass judgment on another.

Judgment of others is what I blame for the problems we face today. That combined with the greed in the world today and the problem is defined. Greed is mentioned several times in the bible also. It is looked upon just as passing judgment is. There should be a lot stiffer penalties for those who steal and lie to benefit themselves. As far as that goes, there should be a lot stiffer penalties for any crime that infringes on another's rights. With that said, I want to say this: there are a lot of things today man has defined as a crime that I'm not so sure qualifies as a crime. There are people sitting in jail right now that probably shouldn't be there. Their only crime was not having the same belief as another man or government. I'm glad it is not a law of mine or a decision I made that put them there. In many cases it won't be the one imprisoned that will kneel before God but the one responsible for their imprisonment.

Laws of God, nature, governments and man all stem from judgment of another or another's actions. Just as our forefathers and the constitution, I am sworn to uphold the laws of God. There is no choice but to live with the laws of nature. Mother Nature does as she pleases and no man has the ability to diminish her power. The laws of governments have been proven to be wrong more times than right throughout the history of mankind. Politicians today have to stand before us and admit their mistakes. It is proven that even in modern times with all the knowledge at our feet, we struggle to find the answers. The law of man carries over into the laws of governments but on a limited basis in the best of circumstances. The real law of man is in our own hearts and minds. It determines how we live our life and who we become as individuals.

I don't have to agree with abortion. I sure won't be the one who judges those who do. Believe in gun control or not, there is now way I will judge either one. I will agree with one side without judging the other. I can disagree with you completely and still allow you your right to choose for yourself. If you do the same for, me we both get our way. Judgment is His. Anytime we decide to judge another it is us that has become wrong. I bet if you take a good honest look at yourself you will be shocked at how many judgmental statements come out of your mouth in just one day. It will never go away completely because some are not capable of seeing who they truly are. Some have been pretending to be someone they are not for so long they actually believe they are who they think they are. I wish I had a dime for every time I heard someone say they aren't judgmental and then say something judgmental in the same breath. If everyone that is capable of seeing themselves for who they really are become aware and focused on not being judgmental we would see a major change in relationships, lifestyles, attitudes, happiness, answers, life, kindness and love.

The title black or white refers to the fact that all these causes revolve around the fact that there needs to be a definite answer. Yes or no, and then all will have to abide by the outcome. Problems, answers, situations and people are all different. Just as people are individuals, so are the problems they face and the answers they need. They don't intend to make a decision on any of these topics. The money is in different sides sending in money to get their way. It's like a new form of business. Start a fight you have no right to start, and then let both sides sign up and send money to fight for their personal opinion. There is no money in the answer or the theory; to each his own. Have you noticed how much is coming into the question? There are millions of dollars disappearing into these battles. For all you know, you are sending your money to a terrorist. Use your money for good causes that support others instead of fighting others. That would be my suggestion.

Almost every battle is over taking away or protecting our freedoms. Well here is a news flash. No one has the right to take away any of another's freedoms. There argument settled! There are no battles, and everyone gets their way. Now, go home and get a job like the rest of us have had this whole time. How dare a man or woman take themselves so seriously that they think they have the right to take another's freedom? The only way to live a life of love and kindness is through tolerance and acceptance. We step backwards in our walk towards God when we choose to judge and condemn. I think it is more human nature than anything. That is why it is so difficult to overcome.

Don't think for one minute that I don't believe in criminal justice. There is a price to pay for the crimes committed against fellow man as well as God's will. An eye for an eye is just as right as turn the other cheek. This is a perfect example of how everything must be determined on an individual basis. There must be one thing that we never forget. Is it a crime against God and our country? Does it devalue everything we stand for? Or are we judging someone just for being different? Are we demanding that free minds conform to know and believe only what we know and believe? One of my wishes for this story would be to get people to see the differences what, why and how they choose to condemn. Maybe understanding that often it comes from jealousy or fear of change. I've seen people that fear all change when most changes are for the better. Change is how we all came to be here today.

As I wrap this story up, the only other thing I can think of to make my point is give a few examples from my own life. Not long after our son was born we experienced a miscarriage. We had two choices. Cry and ask why us as we look for people and reasons to blame, or see ourselves as still blessed and know all things happen for a reason. Be thankful for what we still have and go on. We went on. It wasn't easy at times, but things like that rarely are. A few years later our daughter was born. We would have never known that beautiful girl otherwise. I think he blessed us because we chose to go on. I think it was our reaction to the change in a time when it seemed all was against us that rewarded us later with such great blessing.

An even better example comes through the story of our fire. If we had been the type of people to judge and not treat others the way we wished to be treated we would not have received the support we did. The angels that came to us in our time of need came from all walks of life. Different backgrounds, religions, ages, organizations and ethnicities all came to our aid. We would have never pulled through as fast as we did without each and every one of them. We had no idea the way we accepted and treated others would be what got us through our darkest hour. They say what comes around goes around. We found that out to be very true during this time, and we are very grateful that we are smart enough to spend our time building bridges instead of burning them.

I'll leave you with one more example, and it probably will be the best one for the point I am trying to make. My grandbaby is interracial. Some would have nothing to do with her for that one reason alone. I feel sorry for all those who feel that way because they will miss out on another special person that could add to their life. People's desire to judge without knowing shows little acceptance on their part and leaves little room for growth on their part. I know they don't know God as many others do, and I can only pray they find a way to understanding what life is truly supposed to be about. I had two choices when my daughter first started dating. Be judgmental and racist, forbidding her boyfriend and her to spend time together, or practice what I preached about being open and accepting. It didn't take long to know I had made a new good friend who treated my daughter well. Better than some others before him I might add. Godliness and heart doesn't come in colors or ages. It comes from all places and all types. The quicker one comes to know this, the quicker one can reach a life of true freedom. The longer I live and the more I learn, the more free I become. Free from jealousy, mistrust, anger, pity, fear, hopelessness, loneliness and pain is what we all struggle to reach.

The title of this story refers to options. Not black, not white but all colors. It's all the colors that make the world a beautiful place. Having the option to paint our life in any of those colors is the real answer to a free lifestyle. The only time for conflict is when one takes the rights of another. What one does to themselves is of no one else's concern. It's a time when we can offer our advice and try to help get them back on track, but bottom line is that's all we have a right to do. And even then it's best to proceed with caution because none of us know as much as we like to think we do. I was told by some I should feel betrayed over the situation surrounding my grandbaby. If I wasn't capable of tolerance, I would have never learned the real truth for myself. To be quite honest, without going through the experience there is no way to know how we will react ourselves. All I know is it has always worked out for me when I follow his guidelines. That is the only real advice I can feel confident in giving anyone. Just follow His guidelines and handle every situation that way.

I couldn't have a more beautiful grandbaby. Personally I think she is blessed to have so much heritage and so many abilities. She has the strength of many running through her veins. I said from the day she was born she is special. A year later there has been nothing to lead me to believe otherwise. I look at her today, and I worry for her future. I know if this country doesn't get back to the basic values of God then it is only going to get worse. That is a scary thought when you are looking into the eyes of such a beautiful young human being. We have to start today. It has to start one person at a time. One person can make a difference. One person can make a difference in several different lives everyday. Mainly by exhibiting God's love to everyone you meet or come across each day. I look at that beautiful little girl, and I can clearly see the beauty of acceptance, tolerance and love. It truly is a beautiful sight. I can only hope that you find, as I did, that once you start to control your desires to judge, things get better in every aspect of your life. It truly is God's work right before your eyes. It's like a snowball rolling down a hill. Everyday you will see clearer and clearer. Everyday truly can be a blessing. Everyday you practice this it will get easier. If you are sincere about becoming nonjudgmental then you will start seeing a difference in how you see things and how you react to what you see. Before you know it, you will get to a place where you couldn't judge another if you tried. Imagine what kind of world that would be.

As for me I will make this my number one goal in life. I hope to reach a point someday of being completely free of judging others. All I know for sure is for me, the less I judge the more free I feel. The more free I feel, the happier I am. The happier I am, the happier those around me become. It is without a doubt what got me started in the right direction, and I feel it will be what gets this country headed back in the right direction. I will be the first to admit I don't yet have a perfect record, but where I am today is a long way from where I was yesterday. When I look, I don't see two sides; I usually see many sides. I try to look at everything from every angle instead of just one. Now, instead of looking for black or white, I look for colors and I see many. At the same time, I see how they represent a different perspective instead of a narrow, shaded one. Not only will we get the full benefit of a life without judgment, we, for the first time in our lives, will see the colors more clearly and brilliantly than ever before.

ABOUT THE AUTHOR

I was born and raised in Southern Illinois where I've lived forty-nine years and been married for thirty. I have two beautiful children and one grandchild. I am not a prophet, a poet, a writer, a dreamer or a preacher. I am just one person living in today's world. This is not an autobiography. It is an account of how I came to connect the dots in my search for the truth. I live work and play in the outdoors. Although I have been a carpenter for twenty-seven years, a waterfowl guide for twenty-three years, a ball player for seven years, coach for ten years and a business owner for twenty-three years, I am none of those things. I'm just a man. In my lifetime my titles have included owner, manager, coach, photographer, guide, as well as husband, father, grandpa, friend, writer, painter, producer, editor, pro-staffer, guest speaker, call maker, calling champion, carpenter, lawn guy, and the baby sitter. All those things still only add up to just what I am: one man. One man in a world of many!